AUTHOR	PERLMUTTER, A.	CLASS	956.70441 HIS

TITLE   Two minutes over Baghdad

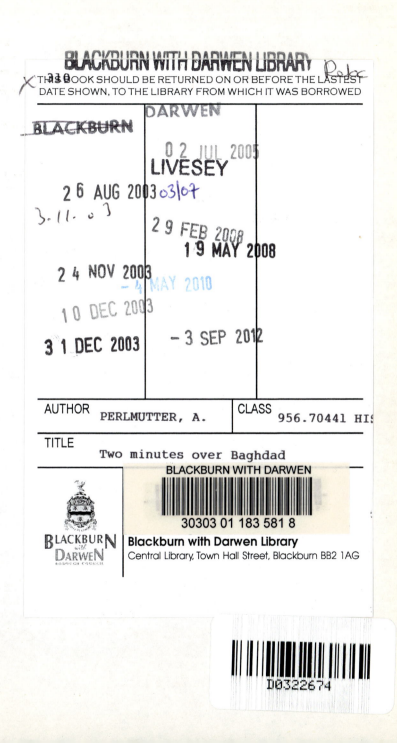

TWO MINUTES
OVER
BAGHDAD

Amos Perlmutter
Michael I. Handel
Uri Bar-Joseph

———

Second Edition Updated by
Uri Bar-Joseph

———

Foreword by
Barry Rubin

FRANK CASS
LONDON • PORTLAND, OR

This edition published in 2003 in Great Britain by
FRANK CASS PUBLISHERS
Chase House, 47 Chase Side, Southgate
London N14 5BP

and in the United States of America by
FRANK CASS PUBLISHERS
c/o ISBS, 5824 N.E. Hassalo Street
Portland, Oregon, 97213-3644

Website: www.frankcass.com

Copyright © 1982, 2003 A. Perlmutter, M. Handel and U. Bar-Joseph

First published in 1982 by Vallentine Mitchell & Co. Ltd.

British Library Cataloguing in Publication Data

Perlmutter, Amos
  Two minutes over Baghdad. – 2nd ed.
  1. Israel. Hel avir 2. Bombardment – Iraq – Osirak 3. Israel –
  History, Military 4. Iraq – History – 1958–
  I. Title II. Handel, Michael III. Bar-Joseph, Uri 1957–
  956.7′0441

ISBN 0-7146-5422-1 (cloth)
ISBN 0-7146-8347-7 (paper)

07/03

Library of Congress Cataloging-in-Publication Data

Perlmutter, Amos
  Two minutes over Baghdad / Amos Perlmutter, Michael Handel,
and Uri Bar-Joseph. – [2nd ed.].
    p.   cm.
  Includes bibliographical references (p.) and index.
  ISBN 0-7146-5422-1 (cloth) – ISBN 0-7146-8347-7 (paper)
    1. Arab–Israeli conflict. 2. Baghdad (Iraq) – History –
  Bombardment, 1981.
  I. Handel, Michael I. II. Bar-Joseph, Uri. III. Title.

DS119.7.P453 2003
956.7044′1 – dc21   2003040915

Printed in Great Britain by MPG Books Ltd, Bodmin, Cornwall

Contents

List of Illustrations

Plates 1–6 reproduced courtesy of the *Israeli Air Force Journal*; numbers 7–11 courtesy of GPO Photography.

Acknowledgements

The authors would like to thank the many Israeli officials and military men who must remain anonymous, for their time and patience in the many interviews they have granted us.

Foreword to the Second Edition

What is most remarkable about the 1981 Israeli raid destroying Iraq's nuclear reactor, so ably presented in this superb book, is that only two decades later could the event's true importance be understood.

While one cannot prove how history would have gone if the attack had never happened, a quite reasonable assessment can be made. Before sketching out the subsequent developments, it is worth showing the most likely alternative course of events.

If Iraq had been able to proceed at full speed in the development of nuclear weapons, it probably would have had several atomic bombs and delivery systems for them in the six years between the reactor's opening and the end of the Iran–Iraq war. Certainly, Iraq was desperate during that period: desperate enough to use poison gas on Iranian troops and against its own people. At minimum, Saddam Hussein would have threatened nuclear retaliation and he might well have carried out one or more attacks to show his seriousness.

With nuclear weapons, Saddam would likely have won the war far more decisively (Iraq can claim to have won the war anyway but the conflict really ended in a deadlock). Iran would have had to accept disadvantageous terms. More importantly, Iraq would have established itself as the unchallenged primary power in the Gulf, while Saddam would have been hailed as the Arab world's leader. He would have fulfilled his ambition to become, in effect, the reincarnation of Gamal Abdel Nasser, who had held such a status as Egypt's leader in the previous generation.

No doubt, Saddam would also have used this position to urge a radicalization of the Arab world. He would have pressed for the expulsion of Western influence, new rounds of Arab–Israel fighting (in which nuclear weapons might well have

been used), and the subversion of existing regimes by his growing masses of followers. Radical Islamism would have been curtailed, but only to be replaced by an equally radical, and far
more popular, resurgence of radical Arab nationalism.

With Iraq armed with nuclear weapons and having defeat-
ed Iran, the Gulf Arabs would have trembled. Saudi Arabia and
Kuwait would have been willing to give Saddam just about anything he wanted. Jordan's King Hussein could easily have been
reduced to satellite status, while Yasir Arafat and the PLO
would have eagerly aligned with the Iraqi leader.

How much would the West have been willing to stand up to
Iraq under such conditions? After all, even with the Iraqi invasion of Kuwait in 1991 there were deep divisions over how
vigorously to respond, both in the United States and in Europe.
An Iraq armed with nuclear weapons would probably have got-
ten away with seizing and annexing Kuwait. Given the heated
controversies surrounding the proposed US-led attack on a relatively weak Iraq in 2003, one can easily imagine how unlikely would have been any Western military attack against a far
more powerful Saddam.

In short, as bad as things were in the Middle East in the two
decades after the Osirak raid, they could have been even worse
if not for the raid: more Arab–Israeli wars, no peace process,
far more upheaval in the Arab world, the destruction or rush
to appeasement of moderate Arab regimes, the wholesale
resort by Europe to appeasement, the deaths of hundreds of
thousands of people, and the United States intimidated into
not responding.

Even this terrible scenario is based on a situation in which
Iraq never actually used nuclear weapons. How much more
terrible would have been the outcome if these armaments had
indeed been fired against the Gulf Arabs, Iran, Israel, or
Western forces?

This is all speculation but it is certainly an extrapolation
based on very reasonable and modest premises. The situation
which provoked a US attack on Iraq in 2003 was made unnecessary earlier by the Osirak raid. If the raid had not taken
place, it would have been too late for such measures long
before anyone in the West was prepared to resort to them.

Finally, whatever the details – the names of leaders, groups, justifications, and the exact timing or target of attacks – terrorism would have been an even more potent threat during the 1980s, 1990s, and into the new century than it was. Stirred by the charismatic and all-powerful leader in Baghdad, convinced that they were on the winning side, and fuelled by a doctrine far more universally accepted than extremist Islamism, Arab nationalist terrorists would likely have sanctified several other days of infamy to rival 11 September as a day of mourning on the calendar.

All these factors make the Osirak raid one of the most important, and formative, events of the twentieth century's second half, with a legacy extending well into the twenty-first century as well. Clearly, too, the attack on the Osirak reactor may well be the most important single bombing raid in history, perhaps save only the far bloodier atomic bombing of Hiroshima in 1945.

Having demonstrated that the Osirak attack was a seminal event in modern Middle Eastern, and indeed world, history, let us now look at the actual context of the raid and the subsequent history of what did take place.

When the Israeli air force destroyed the Osirak reactor, it was still early in the Iran–Iraq war. Iraq's original offensive had been blunted, but the war's outcome was still in the balance and Baghdad held the upper hand. Deprived of a magic weapon, the Iraqis would have seven more hard years of war ahead of them.

In 1982, the determined Iranians, inspired by both patriotism and the regime's Islamist doctrine – in a manner equivalent to how the Soviets fought Germany during their own 'Great Patriotic War' – Tehran's forces forced back the Iraqis and crossed the border. From that point on, the war was fought largely on Iraqi soil. Only at the end did the Iranians finally lose their offensive momentum.

Aside from the heavy casualties, there were many aspects of the war that cost Iraq dearly. Ploughing in huge amounts of money in order to sustain the battle, Saddam wasted assets that would no longer be available later to fuel his drive for regional hegemony. The damage sustained by Iraq's assets and economy would later help motivate him to invade Kuwait. But how much more aggressive might Saddam have been from a more advantageous post-war situation?

Needing foreign help to save himself, Saddam turned towards both the wealthy Gulf Arabs and the powerful West. The former provided billions of dollars in aid, having no desire for an Iranian victory that might have swept them from power. As a result, Saddam temporarily moderated his stance toward them. The United States provided intelligence information and money; the Europeans, especially France, sold weapons. Iraq actively courted the United States and reaped some valuable material gains from this effort, though far less than many people suggested later.

All these factors, however, did more to help Iraq survive than to win the war. Iraq promulgated increasingly repressive measures against the Kurds in the north, a campaign that would lead to mass murder near the war's end. It fired missiles at Iranian cities, with its enemy responding in kind. The newly purchased French planes were used to hit Iranian oil tankers, leading to Tehran's retaliation and, ultimately, to the United States' reflagging and protecting of Gulf Arab oil tankers.

What ultimately ended the war, however, was a mixture of Iranian exhaustion, battlefield setbacks, fear that the revolution was in jeopardy, and an exaggerated concern that the West would intervene on Iraq's side. A key element here was the definition of Iran's war aims. Iraq had attacked Iran, and if repelling that invasion was deemed sufficient, Tehran had achieved that goal by 1982. What helped keep the war going so long was the determination by the Iranian leader, Ayatollah Ruhollah Khomeini, that only Saddam's overthrow and replacement by an Islamist regime would suffice.

Two specific incidents finally helped Iranian leaders to persuade Khomeini to end the fighting. One of these was the Iraqi use of poison gas against unprotected Iranian troops, especially on the southern front, to win quick victories. The other was the shooting down of an Iranian civilian airliner by US forces in July 1988. In Tehran, the reflagging and growing US military presence seemed to suggest that, given their worldview, the United States would try to undo the revolution through direct intervention.

Thus, the war came to an end with Iraq able to claim victory.

Yet this was a Pyrrhic victory if ever there was one. At any rate, the disastrous experience of his attack on Iran did not tame Saddam's ambitions. On the contrary, in the aftermath of the war he redoubled his efforts to take leadership of the Arab world and, in particular, control over the Gulf.

On the basis of his having 'saved' the Arabs from a Persian, Shia, and Islamist conquest, Saddam put himself forward as the model and maestro of Arabism. He revitalized his weapons of mass destruction development programs, threatened to use such arms against Israel, set himself up as patron of the Palestinian cause, and lectured fellow Arab leaders on the need to unite (presumably under his leadership) to fight the menace posed by the United States' genuine victory in the Cold War. All this took place at a time when Saddam did not possess the nuclear weapons that would have bolstered his case, reduced even further his patience, and sharpened even more his appetite.

The 1990 invasion of Kuwait can be viewed as a result of Saddam's relative failure in the war against Iran. The heavy costs of the conflict made him worry about his paper debt to Kuwait and Saudi Arabia, as well as his lack of funds for military efforts, including the still pending question of obtaining nuclear weapons. The burden of battle also made it advisable for him to find some way to ensure the patriotic unity of his diverse population, and to provide them with material gifts based on the looting of Kuwait's riches.

Yet the takeover of Kuwait can also be viewed as a step toward Saddam's ambitions, the first phase of a grand campaign to unite the Middle East with himself as modern-day sultan. One could also consider him emboldened by his purported victory over Iran, at Arab cheering for his deeds, and by Western reluctance to criticize or counter him. If Osirak had never happened, then, Iraq would have been just as likely to have seized Kuwait and far more likely to have kept it.

Given the high stakes, the readiness of Saudi Arabia and other Arab countries to fight back, and the perceived easiness of victory over Iraq, however, a worldwide alliance was assembled to drive the Iraqis out of Kuwait. Again, the construction of this alliance and its overwhelming military victory in January–March 1991 would have been far harder, or even impossible, if Iraq had possessed even one or two nuclear weapons.

The defeat of Iraq made possible a set of serious conditions, laid down in UN resolutions, for Iraq's disarmament, inspections, the payment of reparations, and above all the dissolution of all weapons of mass destruction research programs and the surrender of such arms. In this case, the international community reprised Israel's conclusion when it made the prevention of an Iraqi atomic weapons arsenal as one of the globe's highest priorities.

The Iraqi government accepted these conditions in order to remain in power. Saddam quickly and brutally put down a Shia and Kurdish revolt, which had been inspired by hatred of the regime and hope of American help. While an autonomous zone in northern Iraq was created for the Kurds, Saddam's promises to comply with his commitments basically bought Western acquiescence to his continued total control of most of Iraq and its people.

A complex mechanism was put into place, including no-fly zones, reconnaissance flights, controls and limits over trade, supervision of oil exports, forced reparations payments, and inspections. Repeatedly, Iraq declared that it had turned over or destroyed all its weapons of mass destruction; repeatedly, these claims were shown to be false. During most of the 1990s the game continued. Iraq was certainly constrained and there was only so much progress it could make on developing nuclear or other unconventional arms. At the same time, though, Iraq did everything possible to conceal arsenals and research, to harass and limit the inspectors, and to interfere with overflights.

So relatively successful was the Iraqi effort that only the defection of Saddam's own son-in-law (who was later killed by the regime when he returned home) showed the true extent of the weapons or stockpiles successfully hidden. The details of these events, claims and counter-claims have been hotly debated. But the broad outlines of the story – especially Iraq's consistent non-compliance – are quite clear.

Why, then, did Iraq not comply with its commitments willingly and speedily? After all, Saddam could have sacrificed his weapons of mass destruction in exchange for an end to sanctions, his people's improved well-being, the flourishing of his regime and an end to its international isolation. In such circumstances, he could have then renewed his drive for regional hegemony, including the pursuit of atomic weaponry.

There may be several possible reasons for this. But clearly a critical one was Saddam's continued priority to obtain weapons of mass destruction and especially nuclear weapons, which he had maintained unceasingly since the 1970s. So important was this objective that he was willing to sacrifice an incredible amount of political and economic capital and to take enormous risks to achieve it.

Yet another factor also reduced Saddam's risks. Most of the Western and Arab states were not eager to enforce the sanctions or get tough with Iraq. Resolution after resolution was passed condemning Iraq's behaviour and threatening some response, but action was almost entirely lacking. On the contrary, despite his violations, the sanctions and controls were steadily reduced. Saddam learned that he could do as he pleased at little further cost. Even an Iraqi-directed assassination plot against former President George Bush brought only a one-time, small US bombing raid as retribution.

By the time half-a-dozen years of inspections had been thoroughly foiled and given up on by the UN, Saddam had outmanoeuvred the victors. Saddam had lost far more than he needed and wasted years in the process, but he was keeping his status as Iraq's unchallenged leader, gradually reducing the international constraints, re-emerging as a full member of the Arab world, and developing weapons of mass destruction simultaneously.

All this changed, however, as a result of the determination and views of President George W. Bush, who took office in January 2001, as well as several other factors. Among these was the formulation of a post-Cold War US policy based on its global primacy, a growing concern about proliferation, the search to define a new enemy, and – most important of all – the 11 September 2001 terror attacks on New York and Washington.

In the conception of Bush and his key advisers, Iraq was steadily progressing towards obtaining nuclear, chemical, and biological weapons. The sanctions had not worked, the inspections had been foiled, and regime change was the only hope. But the internal forces opposing Saddam could not hope to bring him down. With the post-11 September war against terror, Baghdad had become a prime target. Bush defined the regime as part of an 'axis of evil'. The US policy of regime change was intended not only to destroy a dangerous radical force, linked to weapons of mass destruction and international terrorism, but also to institute a new democratic order which might have region-wide appeal and break the log-jam characterizing the area.

After giving Saddam a last chance to comply, beginning in late 2002, and despite real domestic and serious European opposition, Bush persisted in his effort. Although the causes of the conflict were complex and controversial, it was clear that an important part of the whole issue was an attempt to finish the job began at Osirak. It was only Osirak that had made Saddam's 1991 defeat, the deterrence of the 1990s, and the counter-strike of 2003 possible.

One final note. In February 2003, on the eve of these dramatic developments, the US space shuttle disintegrated before landing, killing all seven astronauts. One of them was an Israeli air force colonel, Ilan Ramon, who had been the youngest pilot involved in the Osirak raid.

The story told in this book is not only an exciting tale in itself, but it was also one of those events which changed the course of history and determined the ensuing two decades for the Middle East.

BARRY RUBIN
Washington DC, February 2003

Introduction to the First Edition

There are certain events – such as the storming of the Bastille triggering off the French Revolution, or the dropping of the nuclear bombs on Hiroshima and Nagasaki – which act as turning-points in world history. Immediately it can be seen that history has changed course, that nothing will ever again be the same. Other events of historical significance may not be so dramatic, but are still regarded as unprecedented, opening up a new era, a new level of conflict, a new technological Pandora's Box, or disrupting a train of events which before would have seemed inevitable. The Israeli attack and destruction of the Iraqi nuclear reactor south-east of Baghdad at Al Tawita late in the afternoon of 7 June 1981 is one such event.

For the first time in modern history, a successful pre-emptive attack had been made on a nuclear installation. It was not only the first attack on a nuclear reactor (although not fully operative) but was also the first-ever attempt to prevent by force the possible proliferation of nuclear weapons.

The possibility of such pre-emptive nuclear attacks had previously been discussed in other countries. In the late 1940s and early 1950s, for instance, the United States had considered numerous plans to attack and destroy the Soviet Union's capacity to become a nuclear power before Russian scientists translated potential knowledge into actual unprecedented nuclear power – by which time it would have been too late. For some even the mere contemplation of such thoughts was unthinkable, and for most decision-makers the implications of a pre-emptive attack on the yet unborn, undeveloped nuclear weapons programme of the Soviet Union were seen as too frightening and uncertain to pursue. And so the Soviet Union became an equal nuclear power to the United States and the nuclear balance of terror became a factor of life, changing the shape of history irreversibly.

Ironically, history repeated itself with similar results in the mid to late 1960s, when the Soviet Union itself considered and barely rejected the possibility of a nuclear pre-emptive strike to destroy the nuclear weapons research programme of the People's Republic of China. The Soviets even went so far as to drop hints to the United States concerning such a pre-emption – either in order to elicit US support or simply to see how the United States would respond. US diplomats immediately expressed their objections and, while little is known about the subsequent debate among the Kremlin leaders, we do know that the Soviet Union decided *not* to pre-empt and that the Chinese have in time acquired and developed a large-scale nuclear armament programme. No doubt both Pakistan and India have also considered the possibility of launching a pre-emptive attack on the other's nuclear research centres and facilities to destroy their capacity to develop nuclear weapons.

In the light of these precedents the dramatic and historical meaning of the Israeli attack on the Iraqi nuclear reactor comes into a sharper perspective. Yet the circumstances and background of the Israeli attack are very different from previous cases.

Iraq, which lies approximately 350 miles away from Israel, has played a major role in three Arab wars against Israel. It participated both in the Arab League's invasion of Palestine in 1948 and in the 1967 war; in 1973 it sent troops to fight along with the Syrians and Jordanians on the Eastern front. Unlike any other Arab state directly at war with Israel, Iraq consistently and stubbornly refused even to consider the conclusion of a ceasefire or armistice agreement with Israel: at the end of each of their conflicts the Iraqis simply withdrew their forces far back into the homeland and reappeared on the scene whenever a new war broke out. Iraq is, therefore, from both the practical and the legal point of view the only Arab state in a permanent state of war with Israel.

The Israelis have also been afraid of the possibility that Iraq in its apparently irrational behaviour may give a nuclear bomb to a terrorist group, which may in turn use it to blackmail Israel or any other Western state in order to put pressure on Israel. Not only has Iraq been in a continuous state of war with Israel – it has also been openly supporting some of the most extreme Arab radical terrorist groups, Palestinian and otherwise. So much so, that in fact it was declared by the United States to be a country violating international law and a terrorist-supporting state. The US therefore declared in 1975 an embargo on the supply of any US-made weapons to Iraq, even including the sale of Boeing 747 aircraft.

The Iraqi regime was known, in particular since Kassem's overthrow of the Iraqi monarchy, to be an extremely aggressive and irrational one – a reputation enhanced under the leadership of President Saddam Hussein in the late 1970s. Iraq got into many conflicts not only with Israel but also with the Syrian Ba'ath government; it continued its war of aggression against the Kurdish minority; and, finally, in the autumn of 1980, launched a surprise attack against Iran, which curiously enough was never straightforwardly condemned by the UN Security Council.

So the Israeli government had – from its own point of view, and based on Iraq's conduct of its foreign affairs – a legitimate right to be afraid of the Iraqi government's accelerated nuclear programme. To be sure this was a direct threat not only to Israel but also to other neighbouring countries such as Iran, with whom Iraq was involved in war over the Shatt al Arab and Kurdistan (Arabistan); with Syria it was embroiled in an ideological dispute as well as the much more explosive issue of the future sharing of the waters of the Euphrates and Tigris; Kuwait felt threatened by Iraq more than once and in fact was saved by the British from an invasion in the early 1960s; Saudi Arabia was obviously afraid of Iraqi power and expansion from the north and from the threat of Iraqi intervention in its domestic affairs; Egypt was apprehensive of Iraqi leadership in the campaign against the Camp David agreements and from Iraq's aspiration to be the hegemonic power in the Arab world – an aspiration that certainly would have been enhanced had the Iraqis been the first Arab country to acquire nuclear weapons.

Indirectly, the interests of the Great Powers may have been threatened as well by the danger to Middle East, and hence also world, stability. The superpowers have always been afraid of being dragged into a nuclear confrontation and catalytic war by a miscalculation or unexpected escalation of nuclear confrontation between the smaller states. The US and USSR were thus clearly against nuclear proliferation and had behaved very responsibly in their efforts to avoid nuclear proliferation.

This, however, had not been the case with the French and Italians. Both countries were ready and keen to increase their share of business with Iraq (and both had made very large weapons deals with Iraq) and to secure regular supplies of Iraqi oil at advantageous prices (an effort negated by the outbreak of the Iraqi–Iranian War). One way or another the French government, in particular the newly elected Socialist government of François Mitterrand, had good reason to feel guilty and find a good excuse to back out of the project before it was too late.

The Iranians themselves, of course, tried to bomb the Iraqi nuclear reactor on 30 September 1980. They apparently hit the reactor but caused only superficial damage, yet the Iranian attack did not draw so much attention as that of the Israelis nor did it come under such vicious criticism. It is important to remember, however, that it was in fact the Iranians who, though unsuccessful, set the precedent for attacking a nuclear reactor. They were not censured (a tribute to the hypocrisy and double-standards of world public opinion) because they did not official-ly admit it and because they were attacked first by, and were were in a state of war with, Iraq – just as Israel was from the point of view of international law.

The Israelis, therefore, given their fears and experience with Iraq, given their numerous wars with the Arab world and, at the back of their minds, the ever-present experience of the Holocaust, decided to destroy the Iraqi nuclear reactor, which, as we will show, was undoubtedly designed with the primary intention of producing nuclear weapons.

We also describe the less well-known origins of the raid, which was far from being an overnight decision, and Israel's nuclear efforts starting in the late 1950s, which were a means of protecting the Jewish state and changing Arab attitudes towards Israel. We examine the various different stances of the Arab states towards Israel's nuclear project and describe in detail the Iraqi Tammuz project, which was designed to give Iraq a nuclear option – with help from the French and Italians – during the 1980s.

Menachem Begin, Israel's complex, controversial prime min-ister, played a decisive role in the decision to go ahead with

Operation Babylon – as the raid came to be known. 'This will be my Entebbe', said Begin, and as the raid took place bang in the middle of the Israeli election campaign – and considerably improved Begin's popularity in the pre-election polls – many voices were raised, both in Israel and abroad, objecting not only to the raid itself but to its self-serving timing.

We not only examine the decision, the timing and the near-consensus among Israeli political and military leaders that the attack was indeed justified, but analyse what we regard as Israel's chronic phobia – the fear of another Holocaust – through Begin himself, in his youth a Zionist in a Poland where Jews were threatened not only by Nazi Germany but by rife anti-semitism amongst its own people.

Begin, we believe, was genuinely frightened that if he did not order the raid and were then to lose the 1981 election, the Labour opposition leader Shimon Peres would not dare to sanction the strike on Tammuz. Begin foresaw, as did many others, the possibility of another Holocaust, not this time of the European Diaspora but of the Jewish state. We will also examine the personal and political role of Peres, and of one other key figure in Israeli political and military history over the past two decades: the brilliant general and the only strong man in Begin's government of sycophants, Ariel Sharon. Sharon, who at the time of the raid served as Minister of Agriculture, was one of Begin's top military advisors who constantly pushed for the pre-emptive strike on Iraq's nuclear reactor.

But the nucleus of the story is the raid itself and we reveal details about Operation Babylon, analyse the military problems facing the Israeli Chief of Staff, and explain why the option of an air attack was chosen. Months of planning led up to the raid, and we detail the bombing and why and how the Israeli team completely escaped interception, both on their flight to Iraq and on their return journey.

Reaction to the raid is also analysed, not only in Israel and the Middle East generally, but throughout the world, including the critical and, we contend, hypocritical reactions of the US and French government and media. In discussing the raid's impact on the balance of power in the Middle East, we will consider its potential effect on nuclear proliferation all over the world, and forecast the future of a nuclear Middle East.

History has taken a sharp turn – the course and direction of which are always difficult to tell. The best analogy is perhaps to ask what would have happened had British or French Intelligence carried out the successful assassination of Adolf Hitler in 1938 or 1939. No doubt many liberals would have strongly protested that such a deed is against the rules of fair play and conduct between civilized states. But had such an assassination been carried out, World War II might never have broken out and the lives and sufferings of millions of human beings might have been spared.

Yet how can anyone now prove that the lives of millions of people *were* saved by a war that *did not* break out? After all, the particularly cruel and criminal nature of World War II was unprecedented (and unpredictable) in modern history. It is of course impossible to prove the inevitability of something that has not happened.

In the case of the Israeli attack on the Iraqi nuclear weapons programme, the decision to go ahead was taken and the operation successful, but we cannot describe what would have happened had the Israelis *not* taken their action and how the history of the Middle East, the Arab–Israeli conflict and the world might have been transformed.

Amos Perlmutter, Michael Handel,
Uri Bar-Joseph
1982

Introduction to the
Second Edition

More than two decades after Operation 'Opera' – the Israeli Air Force codename for the bombing of Iraq's nuclear reactor at the outskirts of Baghdad – the US war machine is gearing up for a similar but far larger-scale action. In 1981, when Israel carried out its pre-emptive strike, it was the first of its kind. In the introduction to the first edition of *Two Minutes over Baghdad*, we assessed that it was of a historical significance and that it opened up a new era. More than two decades later, this forecast has proven to be true.

In 1981, the international consensus viewed the use of force in order to prevent a future threat of the magnitude of an Iraqi nuclear arsenal as a taboo. As the *New York Times*' editorial defined it, it was 'an act of the inexcusable and short-sighted aggression'. Israel, moreover, was blamed for tearing 'another of the international system's fragile barriers against anarchy' (*NYT*, 9 June 1981). A decade-and-a-half later, a legal study of the raid on Osirak reached very different conclusions. Summarizing the findings of his research, Professor Timothy L. H. McCormack of Melbourne University wrote:

> It had been argued here that Article 51 of the Charter of the UN includes the customary international law right of anticipatory self-defense. Despite the arguments against this position, it has also been suggested that there are limits to the exercise of this right and that those limits are capable of legal analysis. Those limits must be applied to each particular factual situation and, in the case of the Israeli bombing of Osirak, it is suggested that Israel acted

within those limits. Israel faced a nuclear threat which it had tried to remove by peaceful means for several years. It had no guarantee of its own security other than by taking its unilateral defensive action. It had a limited opportunity to remove that threat and chose to do so in a way that required a minimum amount of force with the least loss of human life. This particular use of force constituted an appropriate application of the right of anticipatory self-defense in international law.[1]

McCormack's conclusion radically shifts from the international norms of the early 1980s. In 1981, the majority of experts, including those in Israel, viewed the destruction of Osirak as an unnecessary action, motivated primarily by Prime Minister Menachem Begin's need to demonstrate a dramatic achievement in order to improve his chances of winning the coming elections. Ten years later, in the aftermath of the Iraqi invasion of Kuwait, the second Gulf War, and the 39 Scud missiles that had been launched against Israel during that war, not many inside Israel or outside the country viewed Operation 'Opera' as unnecessary. More than 20 years later, the international community as a whole seems to have adapted the Israeli stand *vis-à-vis* Iraq's nonconventional programmes. The best reflection of this change is Resolution 1441 of the UN Security Council of 7 November 2002, which demanded of Iraq a complete nonconventional disarmament and warned that Baghdad 'will face serious consequences as a result of its continued violations of its obligations'. When Israel hinted, prior to its June 1981 attack, that it might use military means to prevent Iraq from becoming nuclear, the world ignored this warning. More than 20 years later, the meaning of the 'serious consequences' Iraq might face if it does not cooperate is clear to everyone.

When *Two Minutes over Baghdad* was published, less than a year after the destruction of the Iraqi reactor, much of the information concerning the intelligence-gathering and assessment, the planning of the operation, and the way it was carried out were still a state secret. Hence, our ability to tell the full story of this operation was limited, primarily by the strict hand of the Israeli military censor. This barrier has since been removed. Consequently, the first part of the present edition of the book provides a detailed chronology of the way Operation

'Opera' was planned and carried out. This is the most up-to-date description of this operation available in the English language.

Sadly, my two co-authors, Professor Amos Perlmutter and Professor Michael Handel, are not with us anymore. Amos passed away on 12 June 2001, and Michael Handel left us a day later. This edition of *Two Minutes over Baghdad* is dedicated to their memory.

Uri Bar-Joseph
Haifa, January 2003

NOTE

1. Timothy L. H. McCormack, *Self-Defense in International Law: The Israeli Raid on the Iraqi Nuclear Reactor* (New York: St Martin's Press, 1996), p. 302.

Prologue

At 15.00 hrs GMT, on the torpid afternoon of 7 June 1981, the ultra-sensitive infra-red sensors of the US Intelligence satellite in fixed orbit over the Middle East suddenly picked up an unusual signal being emitted above the already overheated sands of the Arabian desert. The IR sensors instructed the satellite's telescopic high-resolution computer-enhanced lenses to focus on 14 fast-moving heat sources flying in two groups only a few feet high above the desert floor. The satellite's sensors were built to respond automatically to any large number of such heat sources moving through the air, and not without reason. This satellite was among those designed to discover and warn of any possible attack from the air against any target in the region.

The telescopic lenses were soon able to differentiate and identify the classic aerodynamic shapes of eight US-made F-16s and six F-15s flying low over the desert in two tight formations. As the lens came fully into focus a scene out of *Star Wars* was immediately transmitted to banks of TV consoles at the US Intelligence HQ. The 14 ultra-sophisticated planes, camouflaged in yellow desert colours, were flying low across the Arabian desert. They appeared to be led by a single F-16 and were evidently a highly organized, disciplined group on a yet unidentified mission, maintaining their mysterious progress to the east. As the two groups advanced, another curious fact was noticed – they continued to fly in complete radio silence, untypical of any training mission.

Below, the 14 pilots, reclining at an angle of 30° in their air-conditioned cockpits (designed to avoid black-out of vision at high speeds) looked straight ahead through their futuristic bubble-shaped canopies and scrutinized the terrain below, passing at an incredible speed, as if they were trapped in some vast, three-dimensional pinball machine.

The sands and bright yellow rocks below them flashed across their eyes against the cloudless, monotonously blue sky. No tree, nor any other form of life was visible. To avoid becoming mesmerized by the never-ending fusion of bright blue sky and yellow sands on the distant horizon their eyes returned to their instrument panels and head-up displays.

Despite the air-conditioning, the pilots sweated profusely, each now concentrating on the panel of instruments in front of him: radar screens, horizontal situation indicators, navigational aids, precision altitude direction indicators, and complex computers and counter-electronic equipment. Each closely watching for any red warning lights. They knew that their lives depended on their skill as pilots, but even more so on the reliability of the complex combination of engines, fuel, electrical wires, weapons systems and every single indicator in front of them. Any human error or the failure of an instrument would mean certain death. At the height and speed they were flying – with the heavy load of fuel and bombs they were carrying – any mistake would also be the last. They would simply disappear, to be swallowed up by the scorching desert.

After an hour and a half of flight, their leader gradually altered course towards the north-east, and, as one well-rehearsed team, they turned in unison their slim but heavy bomb-loaded aircraft to follow. As they continued their progress to the north the terrible noise of their engines spread of miles across the desert. But there was no human – or even animal – life to hear it.

At 17.28 hrs their leader turned his plane steeply upwards. Five other planes followed and disappeared with him.

The other eight shark-like fighters continued their flight and gradually increased their height. At 17.35 hrs they traced a long silvery river gleaming on the horizons, a few patches of green and neglected fields and, suddenly, an immense industrial structure. At its centre they could now make out a peculiar-looking dome. For a moment it seemed as if the structure were actually flying towards them. Then the first of them broke the formation and dived towards it. The rest followed one by one, until again they formed a straight line: an arrow aiming for the heart of the dome.

As they plunged and the first burst of fire, debris and smoke appeared above the dome, their leader could not push away the thought at the back of his mind that this unprecedented attack might change the history of the Middle East and the world. Yet, as he well knew, it was only the last shot in a series of events that had begun almost a quarter of a century earlier.

Operation Opera:
A Chronology of Events

The following is a detailed account of the way Israel dealt with the Iraqi nuclear build-up between its launch in 1974 and the destruction of the *Tamuz I* reactor on 7 June 1981. This description is based on a number of sources, the most important of which is the excellent account of the affair by Shlomo Nakdimon, *Tammuz in Flames* (Hebrew; Tel-Aviv: Idanim, 1993). This is a new and updated version of Nakdimon's book of 1986, which was published in English under the title *First Strike* (New York: Summit Books, 1987). Combined with numerous articles in professional journals and the daily press, as well as talks I conducted with intelligence and military officers who were involved in the preparation of the operation and the pilots who carried it out, the following constitutes an updated supplement to the 1982 edition of *Two Minutes over Baghdad*.

1974

August
The beginning of French–Iraqi negotiations on the sale of a French nuclear reactor to Iraq.

Early December
During the visit of the French Prime Minister Jacques Chirac to Baghdad, the Iraqis make a request for the purchase of a gas-graphite nuclear reactor.

Winter 1974–75
Israel's military intelligence (AMAN) and foreign intelligence service, the Mossad, rank Iraq's nuclear programmes high in their order of priorities, although at this stage the project is not regarded as an imminent threat.

1975

January
Prime Minister Chirac makes a promise, during a short visit to Baghdad, to sell Iraq a nuclear reactor.

April
France agrees to sell Iraq a 70 megawatt (MW) Material Testing Reactor (MTR) of the 'Osiris' type and a smaller, 1MW reactor of the 'Isis' type.

18 November
Following Saddam Hussein's talks in France in September, an Iraqi–French nuclear cooperation agreement – which includes the sale of the Osiris reactor – is signed in Baghdad. The name of the reactor is changed officially from 'Osiris' to 'Osirak'. Shortly afterwards, the Iraqis change the name of the 70MW reactor to *Tammuz I*, and the smaller ('Isis'-type reactor) to *Tammuz II*. The project's name becomes *Tammuz 17*.

1976

January
Infrastructure works start in Al Tawita – the planned site for the Iraqi nuclear project.

15 January
Iraq signs a contract with Italy for the sell of radio-chemical laboratory and three 'hot cells' designed to handle irradiated fuel – the necessary means for plutonium reprocessing. US intelligence sources estimate the reprocessing capacity of the 'hot cells' at up to ten kilograms a year, while Italian experts estimate it at 300–500 grams per year. Israel's main source of

concern is that the facilities would give Iraq the necessary expertise to separate large quantities of plutonium.

27 January
The *Knesset* (Israeli parliament) discusses the Iraqi nuclear project. The Israeli public is exposed, for the first time, to the new threat.

26 August
A new contract, which includes certain changes in the project according to Iraqi demands, is signed with France.

1977

26 February
Israel's Foreign Minister, Yigal Alon, holds secret talks with an Iranian general on possible Israeli–Iranian cooperation against the Iraqi nuclear project. The Iranian response is lukewarm.

30–31 March
Following a series of diplomatic exchanges, in which Israel asked for French clarifications regarding guarantees against military use of the *Tammuz 17* project, a meeting at the foreign minister level takes place in Israel. The Israelis are disappointed with the French guarantees.

17 May
Israeli elections. For the first time in the nation's history the *Likud* right-wing party wins and Menachem Begin becomes the new prime minister.

Early June
Major-General Shlomo Gazit, the director of AMAN, and Major-General (res.) Yitzhak Hofi, chief of the Mossad, brief Begin in a series of meetings about the Iraqi nuclear project. They estimate the project as a source of grave concern. From this stage on Begin ranks the destruction of the nuclear reactor high on his agenda and remains committed to this objective.

Early November
Begin establishes the 'new era' committee, which would deal with the Iraqi threat on a permanent basis. The committee is headed by the Deputy Chief of the Mossad, Nahum Admoni, and includes Brigadier-General Avi Ya'ari, the head of AMAN's Research Department, and three other members. Its task is to estimate, on the basis of intelligence information, the status of the Iraqi project and to find ways to hinder the Iraqi road to achieving nuclear capability. One of its main sources of concern is the fact that at the same time as Iraq builds the nuclear reactor in Al Tawita, another group of Iraqi scientists, headed by Dr Ja'afer Dhaieh Ja'afer, starts working on the design and construction of the weapon itself.

1978

13 January
France informs Israel about its intention to supply Iraq with highly enriched (93 per cent) uranium to fuel the *Tamuz I* and *Tamuz II*. Uranium at this grade of enrichment is suitable for military purposes, i.e., it can be used as an explosive for a nuclear device. The Israeli ambassador in France pressures the French authorities to delay the deal and to replace the 93 per cent enriched fuel with a newly developed low-grade (7 per cent) 'Caramel' fuel, which cannot be used for military purposes. The French reject the Israeli demand as well as similar pressures by the US, Iran and some Arab states.

8 February
Iraq signs a contract with the Italian Atomic Energy Committee and a commercial company (Snia Vicosa) for the build up of the '30 July' project – the Iraqi codename for the plutonium-reprocessing laboratories.

23 August
Begin's first security cabinet meeting on the Iraqi nuclear project takes place. The participating ministers include: Prime Minister Begin, his deputy, Yigael Yadin, Foreign Minister Moshe Dayan, Security Minister Ezer Weitzman and his

deputy, Mordechai Zipori, Agriculture Minister Ariel Sharon, Finance Minister Simha Ehrlich, and two additional ministers. Other participants include the Chief of the IDF (Israel Defense Force) Staff, Lieutenant-General Raphael Eitan, AMAN's Director, Shlomo Gazit, his chief expert on the Iraqi project, Colonel David Bnaya, the head of the 'new era' committee, Nahum Admoni, Brigadier-General (res.) Uzi Eilam, the Director-General of the Israeli Atomic Energy Commission, and a number of personal assistants. The discussion starts with the experts' analysis of Iraq's two options: the plutonium reprocessing and the enriched uranium courses of action. Their estimate, which is also based on intelligence information received from friendly services, is that, in light of the intensive build-up, the nuclear reactor might be completed earlier than expected, perhaps during 1980. The ministers agree that the process should be hindered but are divided about the means to reach this goal: already at this stage, Begin, Sharon and Ehrlich favour the use of all means, including military attack; Yadin, Weitzman and Zipori estimate, on the basis of the intelligence picture, that there is no time pressure yet and that the potential cost of a direct military strike outweighs its potential benefits. The meeting ends with an instruction to delay the Iraqi nuclear programme by all possible means.

At this stage, some staff work on an operation to destroy the reactor has taken place in the IAF (Israeli Air Force), on the initiative of its commanders, initially Major-General Benny Peled and then Major-General David Ivri. Given that the main problem to be solved is the range to the target – over 600 nautical miles – and that air defence around Al Tawita is relatively weak, the most suitable plane for the mission is the Skyhawk A-4. During the late 1970s, the Skyhawk is the only attack plane the IAF operates, which can be air-refuelled (by C-130s) and can carry the heavy bombs necessary to destroy the reactor.

19 October
The French Foreign Minister informs the Israeli ambassador in Paris that the first 12 kilograms shipment of 93 per cent enriched-uranium fuel for the reactor is planned for delivery to Iraq in early 1980.

1979

January
About 150 Iraqi experts start practising various aspects of the plutonium-reprocessing process in Italian installations.

24 January
Foreign Minister Dayan raises the issue of French involvement in the Iraqi nuclear project during a visit in Paris, but receives no positive response.

6 April
An explosion in the hanger of CNIM (Constructions Industrielles de la Meditérranée) – the French company building the Iraqi reactor's cores – destroys the cores of the *Tamuz I* and of *Tamuz II* reactors, three days before its shipment to Iraq. According to all publications, the responsibility for the sabotage lies with the Mossad. The French estimate is that the rebuilding process will take six months and that the new cores will be ready for shipment in October.

1 October
Following earlier negotiations, Brazil signs a nuclear cooperation agreement with Iraq. At the focus of this agreement is Brazilian assistance to Iraq in the domain of nuclear enrichment by centrifuge techniques.

October
Foreign Minister Moshe Dayan retires from Begin's government. He is replaced by Yitzhak Shamir, a supporter of the destruction of the Iraqi reactor.

October
Prime Minister Begin instructs the IDF Chief of Staff to start planning a military attack on the Iraqi reactor. The head of the IDF Planning Department in the Operations Branch, Colonel Giora Inbar, starts preparing ground-based and air-based types of operations. The codename given to the operation: 'Ammunition Hill'.

21 December
According to an updated intelligence report, the first shipment of 12.5 kilograms of 93 per cent enriched uranium is likely to be sent to Iraq no later that March 1980 and will allow the Iraqis to start operating the *Tamuz II* reactor. The report also anticipates that *Tamuz I* is likely to become operational as of July 1980, that Iraq might have 8 kilograms of plutonium by the end of 1982, and that it might be able to produce a first nuclear device by 1985.

1980

18 January
In a meeting at the office of Security Minister Weitzman the pros and the cons of an aerial bombing as compared with a ground attack are weighed. At the end of the meeting Weitzman decides on the air option, although he makes it clear that the situation is not ripe yet for such a strike.

February
Planning for the bombing of the Iraqi project by the IAF gains momentum. The main problems are: the range of the attacking aircraft, which need air refuelling – a complicated and danger-ous action when taken over the territory of a hostile nation; air defence around the target; and the need to rescue pilots if any of them is shot down.

2 March
A report assessing the potential of the Iraqi project as well as the pros and the cons involved in its destruction is submitted to Prime Minister Begin. The report has been prepared by an independent committee headed by Major-General (res.) Aharon Yariv – a former director of AMAN – who was nomi-nated by Begin for this role about eight months earlier. While the report confirms that the goal of the Iraqi project is to achieve nuclear capability, it concludes that, since the Iraqi project is accepted as legitimate by world opinion, its destruc-tion by Israel might lead to some very negative consequences. Specifically, the report warns of the following possible out-comes: an Iraqi attempt to take revenge by attacking sensitive

targets in Israel, including the nuclear complex in Dimona; hostile world public opinion, especially if the destruction of the reactor when it is operational ('hot') causes large-scale radioactive contamination; international sanctions in response to the Israeli breaking of international norms whereby nuclear reactors should not be attacked; intensified anti-Israeli activity in the Arab world; breaking off of the fragile peace process with Egypt; combined Arab military action, with Soviet backing; and damage to the US–Israeli relationship. Begin concludes from this report that the reactor should be destroyed before it becomes 'hot'.

7 April
Following an attack conducted by terrorists supported by Iraq in the Upper Galilee, Minister of Agriculture Sharon suggests bombing the reactor. Prime Minister Begin, supported by Security Minister Weitzman, rejects the initiative.

13 April
The IAF conducts its first exercise aimed at practising various aspects of the planned operation. The attacking planes are Skyhawk A-4 fighter-bombers, which are refuelled in the air by C-130 planes. At this stage, IAF planners finish preparing an operation order that covers the various aspects – such as flight routes, weather conditions, type of bombs and air cover – of the planned operation.

14 May
A meeting of the security cabinet on the Iraqi project. Yariv presents his committee's report, which paints a black picture of the outcomes of the military option and suggests to continue using diplomatic and covert-operations means in order to delay the conclusion of the Iraqi nuclear project. Four ministers, including Yadin and Weitzman, as well as AMAN's new director, Major-General Yehoshua Saguy, agree with these conclusions. Shamir, Sharon and Ehrlich, as well as Begin, reject them. The Prime Minister instructs the continuation of intelligence collection on the Iraqi project and the planning of its destruction.

28 May
Security Minister Weitzman, who objected to the operation, mainly out of fear of the damage it might cause to the relations with Egypt, resigns from the government. The balance of forces within the government starts shifting more clearly towards the military option.

14 June
Yahya El Mashad, a nuclear physicist of an Egyptian origin who now works for the Iraqi nuclear project, is murdered in Paris.

14 June
The first shipment of 12.5 kilograms of enriched uranium arrives in Iraq. It is stored in the *Tamuz II* nuclear reactor. A second shipment is scheduled for early July.

2 July
The first four F-16 Fighting Falcons arrive in Israel from the United States. Originally, the planes had been built for the Iranian Air Force, but as a result of the Khomeini revolution and the cancellation of the Iranian deal they could now be delivered to Israel earlier than expected. Even before the first F-16s arrive in Israel orders are issued to give high priority to their use in a special mission. Now, the IAF commander, Major-General David Ivri, orders testing of its ability to replace the Phantoms and the Skyhawks that had been originally planned to carry out the mission. The main problem at this stage is range. At this stage the planes are supplied without 300-gallon centreine tanks.

Early July
The two squadron commanders of the planned F-16 squadrons, Lieutenant-Colonel Zeev Raz and Lieutenant-Colonel Amir Nahumi, as well as the wing commander of the F-16 wing, Colonel Yiftah Spector, who commands the Ramat David IAF base, are instructed to start practising various long-range missions, in order to reach complete operational status with the new plane by October 1980.

July
Israel initiates a public campaign against the Iraqi project.

Some politicians raise the issue in the *Knesset* and in the Israeli and foreign press, and warn that Israel will react to the looming threat. The warnings fail to reach their goal. French officials make it clear that cooperation with Iraq – which, as they emphasize, signed the NPT (nuclear Non-Proliferation Treaty) – will continue according to schedule.

16 July
AMAN's estimate, as presented to members of the *Knesset's* Foreign and Security Committee, is that *Tamuz I* is planned to become 'hot' towards the following summer. If foreign assistance to the Iraqi project continues according to schedule, Iraq could achieve nuclear capability within two–three years and would be able to build nuclear bombs by the mid-1980s.

17 July
In a meeting between Prime Minister Begin and the US ambassador to Israel, Samuel Lewis, the Israeli premier presents recent Israeli assessments regarding the Iraqi nuclear timetable. The ambassador reports that, according to US intelligence assessments, it might take Iraq a year or two more. Both agree that Iraq is attempting to acquire nuclear capability and that IAEA (International Atomic Energy Agency) inspections would not prevent it from achieving this.

18 July
According to a French 'senior official', *Tamuz II* has become operational.

August
Following the arrival of an additional four F-16s, the IAF commander instructs Raz and Nahumi, his two F-16 squadron commanders, who are to head the two flights, to start practising long-range attack missions. Specifically, they are instructed to find a suitable flight profile, which will enable the planes to reach a range of 600 miles. In order to achieve this goal, they start practising low-speed flights over enemy territory as a means to save fuel. In addition, and in contrast to the US flight manual, they practise dropping the external fuel tanks – which have now arrived – while carrying bombs. Since the planners of the operation assess that the attacking planes would have to

deal with Surface to Air Missile (SAM) batteries and interception planes, they also practise evading such means of air defence, and the conduct of 'dog fights' with minimal use of afterburners, which consume large quantities of fuel. A first model flight of the mission takes place on 23 August. At approximately the same time, arrangements are made in order to assist the pilots of the attacking planes in case they run out of fuel on their way back after the completion of the mission, or are shot down by enemy fire.

14 September
In the midst of Israeli diplomatic pressures aimed at limiting the assistance provided to the Iraqi project by France and Italy, Deputy Defence Minister Zipori publicly warns: 'We will explore all legal and humane avenues. If pressure doesn't work, we will have to consider other means.'

17 September
Iraq declares war on Iran. In light of the danger to the lives of the French and Italian personnel in Al Tawita, most of the foreign staff is evacuated. A number of French technicians remain in place in order to control the damage should the reactor be bombed. In contrast to earlier French commitment, the enriched uranium that has arrived already in Iraq remains without proper inspection.

27 September
Iranian planes attack the Iraqi complex in Al Tawita but cause only minor damage. The planners of the Israeli operation are mainly concerned with the possibility that, in light of this attack, Iraqi air defences around the project will be strengthened.

9 October
Israeli experts meet American colleagues from the US Nuclear Regulatory Commission (NRC) and ask them to estimate the damage a 2,200-pound charge can cause to a reactor after penetrating its concrete protection. The cover for this inquiry is the possible construction of a civilian power reactor for Israel's Electric Company.

14 October

Begin's security cabinet meets to discuss the situation. The Prime Minister, who opens the discussion, makes it clear that he sees no real alternative to the destruction of the reactor by military means. He then allows the experts who are present – among them the Chief of Staff, the head of the National Security Unit at the Ministry of Defence, Major-General (res.) Avraham Tamir, and the heads of the Mossad and AMAN – express their opinion.

Most experts object to an immediate military action. They accept in principle the need to delay as possible the achievement of nuclear capability by Israel's foes, but maintain that drastic action is not yet essential, since Iraq needs another five to eight years (as AMAN's director estimates) to acquire a bomb. At present, when a bitter war is taking place between Iran and Iraq and the Arab–Israeli conflict is not dominating the Middle Eastern agenda, the proposed operation might reunite the Arab world against Israel, increase Soviet involvement in regional affairs, and lead to a US arms embargo. In any event, even if the Iraqi reactor is destroyed, Arab efforts to obtain nuclear weapons will continue – probably even intensify – and, in the long run, preventing them from becoming nuclear is likely to fail.

Those urging an immediate strike – mostly a number of cabinet ministers and the Chief of Staff – maintain that the present time, before the reactor becomes 'hot', and under the cover of the Iraq–Iran war, is the best one for action. Some emphasize that, unlike the Mutual Assured Destruction (MAD) that dominates and stabilizes the superpowers' relationship, a stable nuclear balance of power in the Middle East is a remote possibility because of Israel's vulnerability and the nature of the Arab regimes – especially that of Saddam Hussein. The Chief of Staff warns that Iraq might become nuclear earlier than expected and that, hence, Israel should act now.

In an attempt to reach a cabinet consensus on this critical decision, the Prime Minister does not bring the issue to a vote. He informs the participants that he intends to talk about it with the heads of the opposition Labour Party, Shimon Peres and Yitzhak Rabin.

28 October
Prime Minister Begin convenes the first government meeting on operation 'Ammunition Hill'. After a short introduction in which the chief of the Mossad and the Chief of Staff present their positions, the head of AMAN's Research Department, Brigadier- General Avi Ya'ari (AMAN's director was abroad), presents his assessment. On the basis of the work done in the 'new era' committee as well as by a few analysts in AMAN's Research Department, Ya'ari estimates that the time is ripe for an immediate Israeli strike: the Iranians had recently attacked the reactor twice, using US-made planes, and this might allow them to disguise the Israeli identity of the attackers; the French experts have left Iraq because of the war with Iran; air defence of the nuclear site is still partial; and hostile international reaction to the Israeli strike would reach its height only after the identity of the attacker is known and this would take some-time. Ya'ari and his experts estimate also that many in the West, first and foremost the Americans, would tacitly accept the need to destroy the reactor. On the other hand, Ya'ari notes, fol-lowing the Iranian attack the anti-aircraft defences in Al Tawita have already improved. Moreover, an Israeli attack might cause negative developments, including a crisis in relations with the USA, UN sanctions, a reunited Arab world, a rift in relations with Egypt, and a possible Iraqi response, perhaps against Israel's nuclear facilities in Dimona. Despite the poten-tial negative consequences, and in contrast to the stand of his boss, Saguy, Ya'ari favours the immediate execution of the operation.

The discussion that follows is nonpartisan and addresses the most relevant questions. Begin, who is certain that he has a majority, suggests to vote on two proposals: (a) to carry out the attack in the near future (e.g., during Christmas, when the remaining French technicians are on vacation); or (b) to let the security cabinet decide. Ten ministers support the second pro-posal and six object it. The government gives a 'green light' to the operation. The expectations are that it will be carried out in late December 1980 or in January 1981. The 'new era' com-mittee ends its work.

29 October
Following the government decision, the Chief of Staff instructs

AMAN, the IAF and other IDF units involved, to intensify intelligence collection, planning, exercising and other necessary operational preparations.

6 November
The IAF presents a new operation plan, according to which the attack's sole target would be the reactor. IAF planners assess that hiding Israel's responsibility for the operation is impossible.

7 November
Iraq informs the IAEA that inspections of the nuclear reactor would have to be stopped because of the ongoing war with Iran.

10 November
The new IAF plan is discussed in the forum of the IDF GHQ. The commander of the IAF, who presents it, estimates that a ground raid might be a better option but sees no alternative to the suggested operation.

11 November
According to AMAN's estimate, as presented to the *Knesset* Foreign and Security Affairs Committee, *Tamuz I* is scheduled to become 'hot' in November 1981. However, since the Iraqis are demanding that it be operational by 17 July, it is possible that it will be ready by the end of July.

30 December
Prime Minister Begin informs the opposition leader, Shimon Peres, about the government's decision to bomb the Iraqi reactor. Peres does not express explicit objection to the plan.

1981

January
Intensive planning, testing and training enable the IAF F-16s to fly 600 miles, reach their target and return safe home without air refuelling.

15 March
A cabinet security meeting is held in Jerusalem. The intelligence community is represented by Ya'ari and Admoni, rather than their superiors, Saguy and Hofi, who object to the operation at the present timing. According to Ya'ari, the conditions in January – when the French technicians were out, the anti-aircraft defence was weaker and the Reagan administration had not yet taken up office – were more favourable for the operation than at present. Admoni estimates that the operation can take place even now. The cabinet does not vote again and decides to delay the final decision until April.

Late March
In light of Iraqi pressures to get the reactor operational by mid-July, the number of French personnel in the project increases. By late March, it is estimated at 300 engineers and technicians.

Late March–early April
Following a series of clashes between the Lebanese Christians who are supported by Israel and the Syrian forces in Lebanon, the Syrians use – in contrast to an earlier understanding with Israel – helicopters. The IAF shoots down two of them and, in return, the Syrians deploy a number of SAM batteries in the Baka'a valley. The Syrian move constitutes a breach of an Israeli-declared 'red line' and Prime Minister Begin commits himself to the destruction of the Syrian SAM layout. Supporters of the operation in Iraq express concern that if Israel initiates an operation in Lebanon, it will not be able, because of international pressure, to use force soon in Iraq. Ultimately, the destruction of the Syrian missiles is delayed until June 1982.

27 April
An order summarizing the final details of the air operation is issued. The bombing will be carried out by eight F-16s, each carrying two MK84 bombs. According to the IAF experts' analysis, a total of 16 bombs provides a chance of over 99 per cent of hitting the main target. Hence, although a smaller number of planes could have achieved the mission, but with a smaller chance of success, the optimal number of attacking planes was eight. Air cover would be provided by six F-15s.

Intelligence information received in recent weeks indicated improvements in air defence around the project and the use of other defensive means.

3 May
A security cabinet meeting in Jerusalem. In addition to the nine ministers who make up this body, other participants include the Chief of Staff and his deputy, AMAN's director, the IAF commander, and his intelligence and planning officers, and assistants. AMAN's director reports on Iraqi efforts to improve air defence around the project. The IAF commander estimates that the present plans ensure the destruction of the reactor, but that some planes might be hit. Begin suggests carrying out the operation during May and the majority of the ministers approve this. The IDF issues an order to carry it within a week – on Sunday 10 May.

8 May
The planes planned to carry out the operation and the technical staff move from the Ramat David IAF airbase in northern Israel to the Etzion IAF base, near Eilat. On the way, the F-16s conduct another attack exercise against a target similar to the reactor's dome.

9 May
A final briefing to the pilots in Etzion. Four out of the eight pilots learn for the first time that the target of the operation for which they have practised for months is the Iraqi nuclear reactor. The operation is to be carried out on 10 June.

The Deputy Prime Minister, Yigael Yadin, receives calls from the former Security Minister, Ezer Weitzman, and from Uzi Eilam, who urge him to pressure Begin to call off the attack because there is no urgency to do it now. Yadin rejects their pressure, informing them that the decision has already been made. Later that day, Shimon Peres, the opposition leader, writes a letter to Begin, urging him to call off the operation.

10 May
The Mossad's head meets the Prime Minister before Sunday's regular government meeting and urges him to delay the operation until September, when *Tamuz I* is scheduled to become

'hot'. Begin rejects the suggestion, explaining that in September he might not be Prime Minister anymore, since his chances of winning the election scheduled to take place in late June are not high. His potential replacement, so Begin rightly tells Hofi, is likely to call the operation off, leaving Israel with a real existential threat. In a last attempt, Hofi asks him to delay the attack by two weeks.

During the government meeting, Begin receives Peres' letter. In a meeting with his security cabinet, Begin tells the ministers about his earlier talk with Hofi and the letter from Peres. Fearing that the timing of the mission is not a secret anymore, Begin suggests delaying the attack by two weeks. Most ministers accept his proposal. An order to postpone all operational preparations arrives at the Etzion airbase when the F-16s are ready to take off and the covering F-15s are already in the air. All planes involved in the operation return to their bases.

In light of the fact that the number of the persons 'in the know' about the secret mission has grown significantly during the past 24 hours, a number of precaution measures are taken. One is to change the codename of the operation from 'Ammunition Hill' to 'Opera'.

13 May
A meeting of the security cabinet. Following François Mitterrand's victory in the French elections four days earlier, and his declared commitments to limit French involvement in the Iraqi project and to stop shipments of enriched uranium to Iraq, a number of ministers, including Foreign Minister Shamir, suggest a re-evaluation of the necessity of the operation. Begin, Sharon and the Chief of Staff object to this categorically, and Sharon threatens to resign if the operation is called off. The decision at the end of the meeting is that a committee of three – Begin, Shamir and the Chief of Staff – will decide the date of the attack.

14 May
The IAF Operation Branch issues a new order to carry out the mission on Sunday 17 May.

15 May
An order cancelling the previous day's order is issued.

Third week of May
A new date for operation 'Opera' is made – 31 May. A few days later it is called off in view of a scheduled meeting between Prime Minister Begin and President Sadat of Egypt, who are to convene in Sharm el Sheikh on 4 June. The new target date is 7 June.

3 June
The Chief of Staff issues another directive to the IAF commander regarding the date of 7 June.

4 June
The Chief of Staff and the commanders of the IAF and the Israeli Navy leave Israel to Italy, to participate in the replacement ceremony for the US Sixth Fleet Commander. Preparations towards the conduct of the operation continue in their absence. The Commander of the Ramat David base, Colonel Spector, informs the two F-16 flight commanders, Lieutenant-Colonels Raz and Nahumi, that the operation will take place soon.

5 June
Begin informs the Chief of Staff and the IAF commander, upon their return to Israel, that the operation will take place, as planned, on Sunday, 7 June.

6 June
A special state of alert is declared at the IAF base of Uvda in the Negev, the home base of the covering F-15s, and Ramat David, the permanent base of the participating F-16s. Pilots and technicians are called back to their bases from weekend leave.

7 June
In the morning the participating planes, including the reserve ones, make their way from their permanent bases to the Etzion base – also known as *Canaf* (Wing) 10. At 10:00a.m. a last briefing takes place. In addition to the eight F-16 pilots (plus two reserve ones) and the six F-15 pilots that were to provide them air cover, the Chief of Staff, the IAF commander, and

additional intelligence and operation officers, are also present. The main briefing is given by the leading pilot, Lieutenant-Colonel Zeev Raz. He repeats the well-known routes to and from the target, rescue plans, communications, code words, etc.

The attack was to take place from west to east a few minutes before sunset, so that the sun would be in the eyes of the defenders. In case one of the planes was shot down, the pilot had to wait for a rescue by CH53 helicopters, which were to reach a point halfway to Baghdad at 17:30, when the actual bombing was taking place. The rescue helicopters, however, would not enter a zone with a radius of 25 miles from Baghdad. Each of the pilots would receive 1,000 Iraqi dinars to use in case he had to rescue himself, but all were aware of the slim chance of survival in such a case. Communications with the IAF central operations room in Tel Aviv, known as *Kanarit* (canary) is to be maintained by a Boeing 707 communications command post, airborne over Israel, and an F-15, flying as an airborne command somewhere on the route to Baghdad.

An IAF intelligence officer briefs the pilots about the Iraqi air defence around the reactor. This comprises one brigade of SA-6 (*Gainful*) and additional SA-2 and SA-3 batteries, batteries of ZSU-23-4 23mm and ZSU-57-2 57mm radar-directed anti-aircraft guns, and Mig-21 and Mig-23MF aircraft from nearby Iraqi airfields. Evading this massive defence, depends, as the pilots well know, on their ability to reach their target in complete surprise.

At the end of the briefing, the Chief of Staff and the IAF commander return to Tel Aviv. The pilots start their last preparations, focusing on checking the combat readiness of their planes.

The planes' engines are turned on at 14:30. In two planes there are minor fuel-system problems but the pilots avoid reporting them for fear of missing the mission. A more serious problem is located in the plane of the leader of the second flight, and Nahumi has to replace his plane with one of the reserve F-16s. When ready, the eight F-16s taxi to the start of the runway, where they make a 'hot' refuelling with tankers, so that their tanks remain full until the last possible moment.

Each of the eight F-16s carries two MK84 iron bombs, weighing 1,972 pounds, with a 945-pound H-6 high-explosive warhead. They have about 10,000 pounds of fuel, sufficient to fly to Al Tawita and back – about 2,200 kilometres – with reserve fuel for another 15 minutes' flight. In addition, each F-16 carries two Sidewinder (AIM 9L) air-to-air missiles, chaff and flares. This was a very heavy load; they had a runway of 7,986 feet (2,434m) and were to use most of it.

Earlier, at about 15:00, the rescue helicopters took off and at around 15:50 the six F-15 took off. Each was equipped with four Israeli-made Shafrir heat-seeking air-to-air missiles, four US-made Radar-guided Sparrow air-to-air missiles, and 512 20mm rounds for their Gatlin gun.

At 16:01 the Fighting Falcons started taking off. In under two minutes they were all in the air.

The route to the target was taken at a very low speed, at the height of 300–500 feet. The flight route was not the shortest but it gave them the best chance of evading Jordanian, Saudi and Iraqi radar cover. It also took them out of the range of the Saudi AWACS (Airborne Early Warning Aircraft), which patrolled about 600 kilometres to the south, near the Persian Gulf. They passed south of the Jordanian town of Aqaba on the Red sea and, unintentionally, over King Hussein's yacht. They then penetrated Saudi Arabia over Haql, flew south-east north of Tabuk and then north-east, over the Saudi desert and into Iraqi airspace. Shortly before crossing into Iraq, after a 55-minute flight, the F-16s dropped their wing tanks. About 60 miles from target, over Lake Bahr el Milh ('Lake of Salt'), their fourth and last navigation point, the pilots started final preparations for attack. The six F-15s split from the F-16s, and split again into three pairs, each zooming to 25,000 feet to patrol over a nearby Iraqi airfield, in order to provide air cover against Iraqi interceptors. The F-16 pilots turned on their VTR cameras, armed the bombs, selected all switches for the attack and turned for the final approach. Over the Euphrates river, they turned north-east, on a route that would take them directly to the reactor. Approaching the Tigris river, they entered the ground-to-air missile-defended zone and met light anti-aircraft fire. Here, despite the growing threat, they started climbing to 5,000 feet, in order to identify the target and prepare for attack. For the leading pilot, identifying the dome was the most impressive moment of the mission and a key to its success. Now, followed by the rest of the planes, which were lined up behind him, he started diving towards the reactor's dome at 35 degrees. At a height of 3,200 feet he had the centre of the target in his aim dot. At 17:31, he released the two bombs, breaking to the left, clearing the way for the next pilot.

Delay fuses in the first 12 bombs combined with their heavy mass and a velocity of 250 metres per second allowed them to penetrate the concrete dome into the reactor without exploding, thus enabling most of the pilots to view the target undisturbed by the fragmentation envelope of the bomb, which rises to 2,800 feet. The attack was very intensive. Months of training allowed the pilots to drop their bombs within very short intervals. Some 50 seconds after the first two bombs were released, the last F-16, flown by Lieutenant Ilan Ramon – the youngest and most junior pilot – had released its load on to the target, which was by now covered by fire and smoke. The whole attack took 80 seconds.

Out of 16 bombs dropped, 14 hit the target and only two, the ones dropped by Colonel Yiftah Spector, fell out of the reactor, causing some damage to other installations. The reactor was completely destroyed.

The planes start making their way back to Israel at a height of 36,000 feet. They expect to meet Iraqi interceptors from the H-3 airfield near the Jordanian border, but none comes. In Israel fighters start taking off, ready to intervene if Jordanian interceptors attempt to engage the returning F-16s and F-15s, now flying over Jordan. But no Jordanian Air Force planes take off.

Shortly after the bombing, a codeword sent to *Kanarit* in Tel Aviv informs the military officers present that the mission has been completed successfully without any casualties. The message is delivered immediately to Prime Minister Begin. Since 16:30, his government ministers has been convened in his residence, waiting to hear the operation's results. Now, relieved, they start debating whether Israel should officially take responsibility for the attack. They finally decide to leave the decision to the Prime Minister's discretion.

At 18:40 the F-16s start landing in Etzion. Their mission has been completed successfully.

Shortly afterwards, Begin calls the US ambassador in Israel, Samuel Lewis, to inform him about the operation. Similar messages are delivered to other senior US officials through military and intelligence channels.

8 June
Following reports in Amman Radio that Israeli planes had attacked 'vital targets' in Iraq, Begin orders a release of an official statement on Israeli radio stations about the attack. It is broadcasted at 15:30 by the Voice of Israel.

Operation 'Opera' ceases to be a state secret.

The Middle East

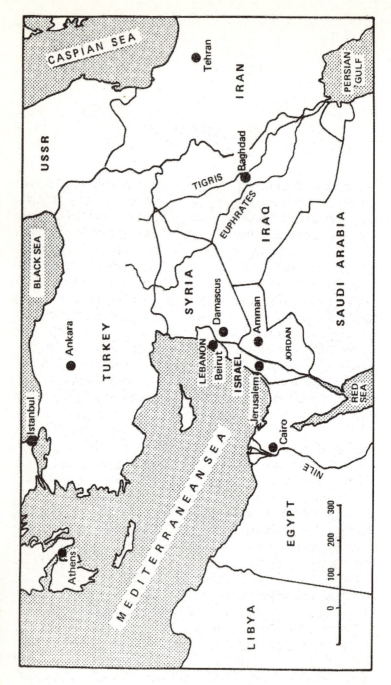

PART ONE

*THE CALL TO ARMS AND
THE NUCLEAR RACE*

1

Ben Gurion's Dilemma

1957

David Ben Gurion nervously paced his office like a caged lion, glaring at the large map of the Middle East hanging on the wall and turned once more to his intimate aides. Yitzhak Navon – later Israel's president – remembers the moment well.

'All night I could not sleep', Ben Gurion sighed. 'What is Israel? ... only a small spot! One dot! How can it survive in this Arab world?' The white-haired veteran, as Prime Minister as well as Minister of Defence for virtually the entire period since Israel's birth in the wake of the 1948 war, had become intimately acquainted with his country's national security. Although not himself a professional military expert, he had his own definite ideas concerning the long-range strategy that Israel would have to implement.

He understood that in the long run Israel's fate might be the same as that of the Crusader Kingdom of the Holy Land which had disappeared at the end of the thirteenth century. Certainly the conditions were not identical but the lessons the Crusaders learnt continued to occupy his mind – in particular in the light of his enemy in the Arab World, Gamal Abd al-Nasser.

The Egyptian President frequently liked to compare Israel with the Crusader Kingdom, and himself to Salah al-Din, the Muslim warrior who had finally eliminated the Christian presence in the Levant. Nasser had reminded his people that the Arabs were endowed with infinite patience. They had waited 200 years to eradicate the Crusaders' stronghold in the Muslim world. If they calculated their moves correctly they would

3

almost certainly be able to drive the Jews out of the region in a much shorter time. Ben Gurion feared that there was more than a grain of truth in the word of the Egyptian Ra'is. How was he to neutralize this permanent threat to the survival of the State of Israel?

Ben Gurion was a hard-core realist: after having tried through numerous channels to engage in a dialogue with the leaders of the Arab world, experience convinced him that they were not yet ready for a radical change in their attitude to the Jewish State. He knew Arab character, and knew that as long as the Arabs were convinced that the Jews could be 'pushed into the sea' they would not accept the existence of the State of Israel as a living entity among the Middle Eastern countries.

One alternative to reach peace that would make Israel secure from the hostile Arab world was to conclude a military pact between Israel and one or more of the Great Powers. However, neither the US nor Great Britain was ready at that time to consider even informal military relations with Israel – let alone conclude a fully-fledged military alliance with it. The reason for this was their desire to build the so-called Northern Tier (later known as the Baghdad Pact), concluded on 24 February 1955, a coalition of Muslim states (Turkey, Iraq, Iran, Pakistan) and Great Britain that was supposed to contain the Soviet drive to the Middle East and the Persian Gulf. A treaty with so many Muslim states hostile to Israel excluded the possibility of any military relations with it.

The USSR itself, as one of the first states to recognize the newly-born State of Israel following its Declaration of Independence on 14 May 1948, and as a supplier of weapons through Czechoslovakia to the Israeli Army fighting for its life, was considered as a potential ally. However, after the British withdrawal from Palestine and towards the end of the War of Independence, the Soviet Union, under Stalin's control, made a radical shift in its Middle Eastern policies and Israel was no longer seen as being capable of furthering Soviet interests in the region. Now, the USSR turned to the Arabs.

In September 1955 the Czech (i.e. Russian)–Egyptian arms deal was made public by Nasser. Israel was shocked. The deal included, among other items, 200 modern bomber fighters, 230 tanks, 200 troop carriers and close to 600 artillery pieces.

At the time it was an unprecedented qualitative and quantitative increase in the level of armaments in the Middle East. In one stroke the regional balance of power was shattered.

The only hope at that critical point in Israel's history was France. The war in Algeria, the help provided by Nasser to the FLN, the natural sympathy felt towards the heroic and lonely struggle of Israel by the *maquis* (French Resistance), and the Suez crisis, all contributed to the development of closer relations between the two countries. It was France which secretly supplied Israel with the necessary weapons for the defeat of the Egyptian Army in its blitz campaign in the Sinai in October 1956. In addition, France consistently supported Israel in the international diplomatic arena, as well as economically. However, following its withdrawal from Indo-China and the Suez Canal it became clear that France was now only a second-rate power. Only a few months earlier, during the height of the Suez campaign, Bulganin, the Soviet premier, sent letters to the British and French premiers, threatening them with a thermonuclear holocaust.

The combined pressure of US and Soviet threats on both the British and French, which forced them to abort the Suez operation, demonstrated their decline in importance in relation to the superpowers, and did not escape the notice of Prime Minister Ben Gurion, who received a personal letter from the Soviet premier which contained, among other threats, the following:

> Fulfilling the will of others, acting on instructions from abroad, the Israeli government is criminally and irresponsibly playing with the fate of peace, with the fate of its own people. It is sowing a hatred for the state of Israel among the peoples of the east such as cannot but make itself felt with regard to the future of Israel and which put in jeopardy the very existence of Israel as a State. (5 November 1956)

Ben Gurion knew only too well that the Soviet threat was nothing more than a bluff, but even now, a year later, he still shuddered at the thought of Bulganin's letter. Even in the aftermath of Israel's victory in the Sinai campaign – the second defeat of the largest Arab army within less than a decade – Arab hostility towards Israel did not diminish. Ben Gurion was convinced that in the absence of some drastic change in the Arab–Israeli conflict this hatred would continue for years to come. None of the Great Powers could guarantee Israel's security in the long run – and only an independent Israeli move of some kind could in Ben Gurion's mind be relied upon to secure Israel's continued survival without external aid.

One such solution was both suggested and supported by two of his most intimate aids in security affairs – General Moshe Dayan, the Chief of Staff of the IDF, and Ben Gurion's close deputy, Shimon Peres. To compensate for Israel's territorial vulnerability and shortage of manpower, these two senior national security advisors pushed towards the development of an independent Israeli nuclear option, which would allow wider room for diplomatic manoeuvring *vis-à-vis* the Arab world and the Great Powers. This big decision was so sensitive that Ben Gurion even kept it secret from most of his cabinet members. But it was to be an irrevocable decision, and since there was no other failsafe way to guarantee Israel's existence and security, Israel would turn to France – its only close ally – for assistance in developing an Israeli nuclear research centre.

In early October 1957 the French government agreed to help Israel lay the foundation for the nuclear knowledge and ability which Ben Gurion saw as the ultimate guarantee for Israel's long-term survival. Shimon Peres, who was in charge of the clandestine Israeli–French negotiations, reported to Ben Gurion that an agreement had been reached.

The nuclear race in the Middle East had begun.

2

The Lion and the Lambs: The Birth of Israel's Nuclear Debate

On 16 December 1960 sensational headlines in the *Daily Express* declared that Israel was in the process of developing nuclear weapons. The report was based on US and UK intelligence sources and discussed the great concern in the West over the possibility of developing nuclear weapons in Israel. Two days later the *Washington Post* reported that from official estimates in Washington (i.e. the CIA) Israel would be able to produce nuclear weapons within five years. The *New York Times* of the same day reported that the Israeli nuclear effort was being made in collaboration with France.

These disclosures upset Ben Gurion deeply. His efforts to preserve a veil of secrecy over the nuclear research project had been to no avail. Between October 1957 and December 1960 hundreds of Israeli engineers and technicians participated in building the Israeli nuclear research centre in Dimona.

But the change of government in France – and the establishment of the Fifth Republic under de Gaulle – was to create a temporary crisis in the special relationship between France and Israel. On 14 May 1960 the French Foreign Minister Couve de Murville had called the Israeli Ambassador Walter Eitan to the Quai d'Orsay and informed him that France would not deliver the uranium promised to Israel for nuclear research by the earlier French government. In addition, Couve de Murville had demanded that Israel should make public its nuclear research. It can be assumed that this change of heart had been initiated by President de Gaulle, who wanted to terminate the special relationship between the two states and improve French relations with the Arab world.

Ben Gurion, for whom this was not only a serious personal disappointment but who now feared that Israel's security would be compromised and damaged, had arrived in Paris on 13 June 1960 for a meeting with the President. The official visit appeared to be highly successful, except for the problem of the Israeli–French nuclear collaboration. A compromise had been reached between the two leaders: Israel gave assurances that it did not intend to produce nuclear weapons and that it would not build a separate plant for plutonium, while the French promised to supply Israel with the remainder of the parts needed for the completion of the Israeli nuclear reactor. It had also been agreed that Israel would publicly announce the construction of a nuclear facility for peaceful purposes at Dimona.

It can be assumed that the French had not taken Israeli promises at face value concerning this highly sensitive area. Therefore, they leaked some information concerning the Israeli nuclear facilities in Dimona to the USA. It seems, however, that the CIA had already known about the new Israeli project. In March 1958, only a few months after the decision was accepted both in Paris and in Jerusalem, the Israelis monitored on their radar screens a plane flying high over the Negev, probably on a reconnaissance mission. Two Mystère IV planes were sent to intercept the unidentified plane and when they failed to do so, Israel operated for the first time its most advanced fighter – the Super Mystère B-II. However, all efforts were in vain, and Israeli pilots could only identify the reconnaissance jet as the famous American U-2. The conclusion for Israel's decision-makers was simple: the CIA had learned about the new secret project. It seems that after Ben Gurion's mission in Paris, the French decided to combine American pressure to their own on Israel, and news of the reactor was leaked to the press.

Ben Gurion now had to admit that Israel was indeed building a research facility in Dimona. On 21 December 1960 he announced in the Knesset that Israel was constructing a nuclear reactor in the Negev in order to contribute to the development of the region. The reactor would be 24 megawatt, its purpose to train scientists for agriculture, medicine, industry and science, so that Israel would be able to design and develop its own nuclear reactor within ten or fifteen years. He emphasized that Israel had no intention whatsoever of producing nuclear weapons. This declaration did not appear to alleviate the US government and Intelligence community's fears concerning Israel's real intentions.

On 3 January 1961 the US Ambassador in Israel presented the Israeli Foreign Minister, Mrs Golda Meir, with a letter listing a set of ultimatum demands in which Israel was urged to explain its plans and intentions concerning the plutonium that would be produced by the reactor, to agree to external inspections of the reactor's facilities, and to declare unequivocally that it would *not* produce any nuclear weapons. Ben Gurion was deeply insulted by the commanding tone of the letter and had a long conversation with the newly appointed US Ambassador. He reassured the Ambassador that the Israeli–French collaboration in this delicate area would be similar to the one that was established between Canada and India, or any other unilateral nuclear collaboration agreement. Any plutonium produced by the reactor would be returned to the country supplying the enriched uranium. At the same time Ben Gurion expressed his objection to foreign inspection of the reactor. 'We are not interested in any hostile states meddling in our internal affairs,' he explained to the young ambassador. On the other hand he was ready for an American or any other friendly state visit to Israel's nuclear facilities, but not in the near future – only after a relaxation of the excitement created following the disclosure of Israel's nuclear project.

Growing American pressure revived the internal debate in Israel concerning the desirability of achieving nuclear independence. Cabinet members and party colleagues – still ignorant of their own country's nuclear programme – began to express their own opinion on the matter. Ben Gurion came under cross-fire from his domestic adversaries as well as international friends and foes. Members of his ruling party Mapai, such as Eshkol, Golda Meir and Sapir, expressed their objections to his decision to develop a nuclear option for Israel. Eshkol and Sapir, both economic experts, were afraid of the enormous costs of this project. Golda Meir, for many years an enemy of Peres, based her objections to the project more on personal than on logical and objective reasons.

Thus in the early 1960s the Israeli political elite became divided over Israel's nuclear policies. The question was: on

what would Israel rely during the next decade, a strong conventional army primarily based on tanks and tactical aircraft or
on 'the forecasted technologies of the 1970s', as the pro-
nuclear parties in Israel's security community euphemistically
referred to Israel's nuclear programme?

Dayan and Peres found themselves in a minority in the ensuing debate. Yigal Allon, the former commander of the
'Palmach' and one of the most original and brilliant Israeli military minds, brought a number of strong arguments against
them.

It seems that, faced with these external pressures, as well as
other domestic problems, Ben Gurion decided to retire and
leave the rest of the job to the younger generation. It was a hard
decision for him. For many years he had cleverly navigated
Israel through political storms and crises, using his political
instincts. His aim had always been to bring Israel to a safe port,
but like Moses, he was not to reach that Promised Land. And
although peace with the Arabs was by no means promised, Ben
Gurion still hoped that the nuclear infrastructure laid down by
him and his aides would be a safe guarantee against any Arab
drive to destroy the country of Israel, and that by achieving a
nuclear option, a balance of terror would be created in the
Middle East, thus leading to peace.

But the developments that were to follow put an end to such
hopes.

3

Nasser's Nightmare, Sadat's Solution

For Nasser's Egypt, as well as for Ben Gurion's Israel, the nuclear question became (like other elements of the Arab–Israeli confrontation) a purely 'zero-sum game', an all-or-nothing question. Nasser's ambitions were to liquidate the Jewish state and to rub its name off the Middle East map, as a means to reach Arab unity under his control. If Israel were to acquire the bomb it would thwart this and in order to neutralize such a threat to his aims, Nasser tried out certain countermeasures.

At the beginning of 1961, immediately after the Israeli efforts leaked out, Nasser convened the 'Arab Advisory Commission of Military Affairs'. This consisted of all the chiefs of staff of the Arab armies and its aim was to provide Nasser with a scheme for a pre-emptive strike against the Israeli reactor in Dimona. Nasser himself admitted as much to a conference that met at the time because he 'was worried about the development of nuclear Israeli weapons'.

But this was not enough for the ambitious Egyptian president. He realized that it would take the divided Arab world at the height of the 'Arab Cold War' many more years before it would be ready to unite in a war against Israel. Nasser felt that he had to act immediately in order to create a counter threat which could, according to his philosophy, neutralize the new Israeli atomic threat.

By the end of 1959 an Egyptian effort to build supersonic warplanes and surface-to-surface missiles had already started. Hundreds of German scientists, mainly Nazi veterans, were mobilized to work in Egypt in three top-secret projects. The first was called Project 36. Willi Messerschmitt – the famous

11

father of the ME109 of World War II – was busy building a new type of plane for the Egyptian dictator, named HA300. In the second project, codenamed 135, Ferdinand Brandner headed a group of German and Egyptian engineers and technicians who tried to develop a jet engine for the fighter built by the first group. The most secret project was called 333 or 'thalathat' in Arabic. In this plant medium-range surface-to-surface missiles were built. Their range was supposed to be between 280 and 580km, or, as Nasser put it in one of his speeches, they could hit every target south of Beirut.

It seems that when Nasser found out about the Israeli activities in Dimona, he decided to change his plans a little. Before, he had planned to arm the warheads of his missiles with conventional explosives. Now he decided to go into new projects which would supply him with unconventional warheads. The first project was called Ivis I, the second Operation Cleopatra.

Ivis I was supposed to supply the missile warheads with new dangerous materials: Cobalt 60, a radioactive isotope which would spread deadly radiation over vast areas of Israel. Other alternatives, such as chemical or biological materials, were considered as equally fitting to this aim.

The second project was aimed at supplying nuclear warheads as a counterthreat to the supposed Israeli atomic bomb. Since Egypt had no nuclear reactors by that time, or at least no reactors with the capacity to supply weapon-grade materials, Egypt intended to buy low-grade uranium in the free international market and enrich it by using new special techniques of centrifuge developed in West Germany and Holland.

But neither independent Egyptian efforts nor Nasser's efforts to reunite the Arab World succeeded. Arab rulers, though worried about the Israeli bomb, were not ready to put their armies under Egyptian command: they knew the ambitious president and were sure that first of all he would undermine their regime and only then would he turn to deal with the Israelis.

Israel, for its part, started a highly secret operation against the German scientists working for Nasser. By the end of 1962 letters started exploding in the hands of the top engineers of project 333. Dr Krug, one of the main organizers of the jet engines plant, disappeared and has not been traced to this day.

All those involved in the secret Egyptian projects were now in fear for their lives. The long, experienced hand of the Israeli Mossad was in full operation again, combined with secret efforts made by the Israeli premier – Ben Gurion – to convince his German colleague Adenauer that the German scientists should stop working for Nasser's deadly projects.

The intelligence operation, together with Israel's diplomatic efforts in West Germany, was fruitful. Although the Egyptians had by the mid-1960s built up a number of models of SS missiles, such as Al Caher, Al Za'afer and Al Nasser, they were found to be unreliable in launching procedures and very inaccurate. They never reached the stage of combining the warheads with the missile itself. Nasser's ambitious plan proved to be unsuccessful after years of hard work and highly expensive investments.

These failures had not prevented Nasser from trying to stop the Israeli nuclear project. In the middle of the 1960s, while a secret debate was going on in Israel over the big investments needed for the secret project, Nasser did try his third alternative. Mohamad Hasnein Haikal, the editor of *Al Aharam* and a close friend of the Egyptian president, recounted in his memoirs how Nasser tried to recruit from certain top leaders of the world, including Mao Tse Tung and Leonid Brezhnev, ready-made nuclear weapons. But these efforts proved to be a failure too and Nasser grew more frustrated than ever.

His last alternative was more successful. He asked Brezhnev and other Kremlin leaders to give Egypt nuclear guarantees should Israel acquire its A-bomb. *The New York Times* of 14 February 1966 reported from Cairo that the Deputy Defence Minister of USSR, Andrei Grechko, gave Egypt certain nuclear guarantees, but by that time no one could ascertain what sort of guarantees they actually were.

It is not yet clear whether Nasser moved his troops into the Sinai desert in May 1967 as a step towards a pre-emptive strike against Israel's nuclear facilities or for other reasons. But there could have been absolutely no logic in his actions unless this was one of his main aims. It is known that just a day or two before the war started Nasser started blackmailing Israel and demanded the southern part of the Negev, which connects

13

Israel to the Red Sea. His intention was probably to blackmail Israel in the nuclear field as well. Without taking this into account, no one can explain logically Nasser's behaviour on the eve of the Six Day War.

It would be wrong to consider Nasser as the only Arab ruler to be disturbed about the Israeli nuclear threat. Speeches and declarations on that issue were again and again made by all Arab statesmen and politicians. Even the PLO, still at that time only a small organization, depending on Egyptian, Syrian and Jordanian goodwill, was concerned.

In May 1966, Ahmed Shukeiri – the then PLO leader – gave a speech at the opening ceremony of the Third Palestinian National Committee which took place in the Gaza Strip. Among other items the Israeli efforts in Dimona were discussed. The Palestinian leader said that the Arabs must prepare for a pre-emptive war against Israel before the Jewish state became nuclear. In the final declaration of this third conference, was one paragraph warning the Arab states of the Israeli A-bomb. Israel's aim, according to this paragraph, was to create division in the Arab world and to conquer more Arab territories.

One can understand the psychology that created Nasser's special tough resistance to Israel's nuclear project. Most of its population is concentrated in the Nile Valley and the Nile Delta. Any infection of the river's waters with radioactivity could bring an end to Egypt's long history. An Israeli A-bomb exploding over the Aswan Dam would cause a destructive fluid which would carry with it all the villages of the Delta area as well as Cairo itself.

One can also understand the worries of the Palestinians. Israel holding the A-bomb is a status-quo state that nobody will ever be able to drive out of the Middle East. Ben Gurion had no intention of enlarging the Israeli territory, and the Israeli efforts were not to change the status quo, but to maintain it, and the Palestinians were predominantly worried about this.

In the middle of the 1960s, Arab conventional forces had no capability to attack the Israeli facilities in Dimona. Their defeat in June 1967 had probably taught Nasser, Hussein and the rest of the Arab leaders some tough lessons. The most important of them all was that any attempt to win a war against Israel by conventional means would almost certainly be doomed to failure. An alternative course was a long war of attrition on the new borders of the Suez Canal, the Golan Heights and the Jordanian valley. In the Egyptian and Syrian borders the war was carried out mainly by regular armies. In the Jordanian valley, as well as in the occupied territories, the PLO was the IDF's main enemy. Neither in conventional war nor in a struggle of attrition did the Arabs succeed in achieving their aim, the IDF had many casualties, but Israel did not give up the new territories it had acquired in the 1967 war.

The end of the war of attrition and Nasser's death in the summer of 1970 created a new situation in the Arab–Israeli conflict. Sadat – Nasser's successor – had a different view of Middle East relationships. He did not want to renew the war of attrition on the banks of the Suez Canal in the way it had been between 1969 and August 1970. Instead he preferred to launch a massive surprise attack that might bring limited military achievements, but maximum political gains.

In Egypt itself a serious debate had been going on since Sadat had come to power over how the Israeli nuclear threat should be treated. The pro-Soviet faction, including Ali Sabri, Ahmed Sidki, Hasnein Haikal and others – all military men or influential ones – demanded an aggressive independent Egyptian nuclear policy or at least solid Soviet nuclear guarantees.

Anwar Sadat's point of view was different. He understood that there was little chance of achieving an independent nuclear umbrella for Egypt and that he would never be able to obtain Soviet nuclear devices positioned on Egyptian soil, with combined Egyptian–Soviet control. On the contrary he could read only too well the signals that had been coming from Israel ever since the day he had come to power. Dayan and others in Israel hinted that any Arab attempt to attack Israel beyond the 1967 lines into the heart of the country would face an Israeli counterattack. The president's conclusion was that a nuclear threat did not apply to an Arab attempt to conquer at least part of those territories which had been occupied by the Israelis since 1967.

With this in mind, he planned his surprise attack against Israel in 1973. It is still not clear yet whether, in his preplanning, he had co-ordinated a Soviet nuclear umbrella as a deterrent to, in his opinion, a possible Israeli nuclear reaction.

From what can be judged about the Soviet behaviour during the war and especially towards its end, it is fair to assume that there was such a co-ordination. By 23 October, a Russian cargo ship carrying nuclear warheads had arrived in Alexandria. It was probably a quick response to the Israeli threat of 9 October which was detected by Soviet satellites who observed from space every move in Israel. Another explanation was that this may have been a rumour deliberately spread by the United States to bring pressure on Israel to conclude the war.

From Sadat's point of view, the October war should be seen in terms of Clausewitz's dictum: 'War is the continuation of policy by other means'. After the Egyptian Ra'is had realized that all diplomatic efforts would lead to a dead end, he decided to try a limited military option which, combined with an oil embargo, would lead to a significant Israeli withdrawal from Arab territories. And since in the war itself Egypt would not be threatening Israel's existence – although Dayan for one saw it as such a threat – Sadat saw no nuclear danger for Egypt or Cairo.

Since the 1973 war Egypt had been preparing long-range plans to operate nuclear-powered electricity stations. Egypt had no nuclear facilities for producing a bomb. It had one 2-megawatt research reactor in Einshas. The Soviets, who supplied Egypt with this WW R-C type reactor at the end of the 1950s as well as a small laboratory-scale reprocessing plant, no longer operated this project and it now served to train Egyptian scientists in nuclear physics. Throughout the Arab world no other state has reached Egyptian standards in terms of qualified personnel and expertise. Following the October war, however, Egypt was involved in a very ambitious programme to build nuclear power stations – more than 20 American-, German- and French-made nuclear-powered stations were planned for Egypt. Egypt declared repeatedly that it was against the introduction of nuclear weapons to the Middle East. Its 'Atom for Peace' programme combined very well with this policy, as well as with Sadat's policy towards Israel after 1973.

The Egyptian president's trip to Jerusalem in November 1977 was one of the biggest surprises in the history of modern world diplomacy. And there is no doubt that one of the greatest factors that motivated Sadat to choose this direction in policy was the Israeli nuclear threat. (In the long-running negotiations between Israel and Egypt, the nuclear issue had been paramount – although both sides, including the Americans, were reluctant for the world's media to publicize it.) Egypt was far too vulnerable and the president did not want to take any more risks. Sadat therefore surrendered all hopes of destroying the Jewish state. But staying in the conflict without getting back the Sinai desert, which had been occupied in 1967, and still investing large amounts of money in an army which was supposed to confront Israel, was not proving to be a good policy for Sadat. He had to choose a new line, otherwise any crisis in the delicate relations between his country and Israel would again bring about the threat of nuclear catastrophe.

In Egypt, the bitter debate over the pros and cons of an independent Egyptian nuclear option continued. Those who supported it, headed by Minister of Foreign Affairs Ismail Fahmi, insisted that Egypt should not sign the Nuclear Non-Proliferation Treaty (NPT) and that it should acquire independent nuclear status if it wished to keep its role as a leading state in the Arab world. It seems that Fahmi and his supporters were worried about a nuclear Middle East in the 1980s. Israel and at least one Arab state (probably Iraq) would have the bomb. Without nuclear status, Egypt would probably lose much of its ability to influence Middle East policies. In any case if Egypt signed the NPT it would freeze the situation and even in the future the Israelis would be able to blackmail the Egyptians: clearly an unacceptable situation for Fahmi and his group.

Israel's capacity to blackmail Egypt also troubled Sadat in the peace negotiations. Flora Lewis, *New York Times* reporter, reported on 2 December 1977, a short time after Sadat's visit to Israel and three days before Sadat met Begin in Ismailia, that Egypt would require Israel to surrender its nuclear arms as part of a final peace agreement. But Israel was to find it impossible to accede to this demand, because of Iraqi efforts in this field. On 8 November 1978 it was reported in the same paper, that Israel had rejected two Egyptian offers to give up the nuclear arms race in the Middle East and to limit the conventional arms race on the same grounds. Israel had still to deal with the nightmare of the so-called 'Eastern front', comprising Syria, Jordan and Iraq, and supported by other Arab states.

4

The Quest for the Muslim Bomb: Libya, Syria, Saudi Arabia and Pakistan

One of the most prominent Arab rulers from the 1970s has been Libya's president, Muamar Gaddafi. Since he came to power in 1969 in a successful coup against King Idris, the young Libyan colonel has acquired the reputation of being one of the world's most irresponsible and extremist leaders.

Gaddafi sees himself as the Islamic successor of Colonel Nasser. His intellectual world is very simple and is described in his 'Green Book' – an imitation of Mao's Red Book. According to Gaddafi, two major theories concerning state systems were introduced and have failed since the nineteenth century: Communism and Capitalism with all their various branches. Gaddafi proposed a new theory: the way of Islam and the Koran, in which one can find the best of both worlds. A combination of equality of rights, simplicity, modesty and morality. Gaddafi's approach is militant and aggressive. He believes that the Koran theory should be adopted throughout the world, not by persuasion, but by force. His aims justify his means absolutely, and in this sense the use of force, compulsion and even international terrorism, are all legitimate means.

For the intelligent Western reader, such methods would seem to destroy international order, and the murder of political enemies in London or Paris, the subsidizing of terrorist acts like the murder of eleven Israeli athletes in the Munich Olympic games of 1972, or collaboration with international terrorists like the famous Carlos, all seem incomprehensible. But for Gaddafi these are legitimate acts in his efforts to establish the pure Islamic way throughout the world. Since Gaddafi has no scruples and – more crucially – Libya has so much oil, he became one of the most dangerous figures in the Arab world.

His first attempts to obtain nuclear weapons seem a little pathetic today. The young Libyan leader went to Nasser at the beginning of 1970 with a demand to start a full-scale war against Israel. When Nasser, and then Sadat, explained to him that such a move would be impossible because of the hidden Israeli nuclear threat, Gaddafi decided that his holy duty would be to neutralize the Israeli advantage by the production of an Arab A-bomb. Through mediators he asked Chou En-lai of Red China to sell him nuclear devices. The Chinese statesman found it difficult to make the inexperienced, fanatical leader understand that nuclear bombs are not sold on the international free market: the young colonel had to return from China with empty hands.

Failing to obtain a ready-made A-bomb 'off the shelf', as it were, Gaddafi embarked on a longer but more promising route. For years he was to negotiate with the USSR for the sale of a nuclear reactor. Although the Soviets supplied him with their best conventional weapons, they were naturally suspicious of such a sale, but in 1973 an agreement was reached and the USSR sold Gaddafi a 10-megawatt research reactor, now situated in Siobu Bay on the Libyan coast. The Soviets also agreed to supply Gaddafi with a 440-megawatt nuclear power plant.

Taking into account the low grade of manpower in Libya and the lack of nuclear scientists in the country, together with its oil surplus, one must conclude that Gaddafi tried to acquire a nuclear option by using Soviet support. But the Soviet Union always faithfully observed the NPT rules, which seek to limit the spread of nuclear weapons throughout the world, and it never enabled Libya to use its own reactors for this purpose.

But Gaddafi chose a third and even more reliable alternative. There is now abundant evidence to indicate that Gaddafi subsidized the Pakistani nuclear effort by more than $1,000 million. Although the debate goes on regarding the exact amount funded, it is clear that there was co-operation and collaboration between the two states. Pakistani technology seemed to have reached the highest level in the Muslim world and it became the first to have the 'Muslim Bomb'. Gaddafi, in the light of all his failures in the past, wanted to make sure that he would not lose his investment in Pakistan.

To this end, Libya bought as much uranium as it could from Niger – possibly the world's leading supplier – and part of this went to Pakistan. Although Pakistan tried to buy the raw materials direct from Niger, its ruler preferred to sell them to Gaddafi. By accumulating thousands of tons of uranium ores, Gaddafi more or less controlled Pakistan's nuclear effort and it thus seems that he had a good chance of obtaining the bomb, if and when Pakistan manufactured it. But history has proven that Gaddafi was mistaken again. Pakistan built the bomb, but Libya, despite its assistance to the Pakistani nuclear project, has remained without any nuclear capabilities until the present day.

Other Arab states in the Middle East besides Iraq have shown interest in the nuclear field, but at this stage there are no clear signs that they are seriously intending to acquire the bomb.

Syria is a classic example, on the one hand showing interest in achieving a nuclear option, on the other doing almost nothing to achieve it. In an interview given by then Syrian President Assad on 29 April 1978 to the Lebanese *paper A'Nahar Al Arabi Wa' Dawli*, he said, 'Syria has a fully detailed counter plan, in case Israel acquires a bomb.' From what other leaders of the Syrian Ba'ath party have said, one can understand that Syria will never negotiate a peace treaty with Israel as long as the Jewish state has nuclear superiority. Like Fahmi and others in Egypt, the Syrians seemed in the late 1980s to be worried about Israel using its nuclear option as a card on the negotiating table. The Syrians therefore have two obvious alternatives: to produce a Syrian nuclear bomb; or to continue the status quo and to resist negotiations.

In April 1978, President Assad took the first option while visiting India, attempting to reach an agreement for nuclear co-operation between the two states. India had one successful nuclear test in 1974 but declared that it had no intention of reaching independent nuclear status, nor did it like the idea of military collaboration with Syria in the atomic field. French intelligence sources let leak that this was Assad's second failure: a few months earlier France had given him a negative answer as well.

After the raid on the Iraqi reactor in June 1981, Syria renewed its efforts. At the end of June 1981 the Minister for Electricity Affairs, Omar Joseph, visited Belgium. He negotiated a contract with various Belgian and Swiss companies to build nuclear-powered electricity plants. The deal appears to have involved six reactors with a total power of 600 megawatts. In view of the Israeli raid, the Syrian minister emphasized that the deal had no military aspects. But given Syrian efforts to balance its nuclear capacity with that of Israel, there is no doubt that if this deal had taken place, it could have had significant military aspects.

Ultimately, the Syrians gave up their nuclear ambitions. Though it is possible that they received some latent nuclear guarantees from the Kremlin in the early 1980s, the collapse of the Soviet Union left them facing the Israeli threat without external help. The solution Damascus found to this dire situation was similar to that adopted by other Third World counries: a massive build-up of a chemical and biological arsenal, in part as a means to arm its large stock of Scud surface-to-surface missiles.

Saudi Arabia has also shown interest in nuclear reactors. Since it is clear that this oil kingdom has no problems in supplying itself with energy, it is quite obvious that its top leaders are interested mainly in the military aspects of the project.

On 24 April 1979 the *Christian Science Monitor* reported that, as a result of advances in the Iraqi nuclear project, the Saudis were interested in a similar project. In May 1973, King Khaled paid a visit to France and signed an arms deal contract worth $3 billion. After the visit, it transpired that the King was very interested in implementing French reactors on Saudi soil.

In July 1979 it was revealed that as early as 1975 a secret deal had been signed between France and the Saudis to supply the latter with a French reactor. *Al Hawadath*, a Lebanese pro-Saudi paper known for its good sources in Saudi reported on 20 July 1979 that the Saudis took over the French firm Creusot Loire, the military section of Amban Schnider which manufactures nuclear reactors.

In the late 1970s and the early 1980s, when the Israeli decision-making process concerning the Iraqi nuclear project was underway, it seemed that the Saudis might pursue a nuclear option as well. And if this was so, the main reason for the Saudi change of policy must have been the Iraqis. Since Saudi Arabia has always been a status quo power in its domestic and foreign policy, it tried to keep the Middle East denuclearized. The rulers of Saudi Arabia know that to develop an A-bomb they will have to reach a high standard of manpower capable of producing the bomb. Such a group of young, intellectual and technologically-minded people would naturally be a threat to the ruling family. In this sense, the Saudis will always prefer the present situation in the Middle East, without a new nuclear arms race, and one can assume that, more than any other state in the Arab world, Saudi Arabia profited from the Israeli raid.

But the first Islamic state to manufacture the bomb would not be an Arab one, but one that has never taken any active part in the Arab–Israeli conflict – Pakistan.

In January 1972 a secret conference was held in Multan – a small town in the south-eastern desert of Pakistan. Zulficar Ali Bhutto – the then Pakistani premier – had been shocked by the results of the last war between his country and India, and brought all his top nuclear scientists to this meeting. 'Can you supply me with the bomb?' he asked the group of fifty who were discussing the subject with him. The answers were positive. Bhutto was very satisfied and promised to supply his scientists with everything they needed.

In February 1974, the first conference of Islamic states took place in Pakistan. Most of the world's attention was focused on the oil embargo and other such issues. But behind the scenes Bhutto negotiated a deal with Colonel Gaddafi, and in this top-secret agreement Gaddafi agreed to subsidize part of the Pakistani efforts to acquire an A-bomb. Pakistan agreed to supply the Libyans with the equipment and expertise in order that the Libyans would be able to build the bomb in Pakistan. Colonel Gaddafi explained that he preferred all Libya's nuclear efforts to be concentrated in Pakistan, because Israel would never let an Arab Middle Eastern state produce a nuclear device on its own soil.

In May 1974, India exploded 'a nuclear device for peaceful purposes'. The Indians were using the same reactor as the

Pakistanis: a Canadian 'Candu' type owned by both states at the beginning of the 1960s. This reactor is unique: its by-product is plutonium and it has a remote control system which enables scientists to insert and remove uranium capsules without interrupting the reactor's performance.

The USA became very worried over the possibility of nuclear war between India and Pakistan. Secretary of State Kissinger pressed Pakistan and France to cancel a deal by which France was to supply Pakistan with a plutonium-processing plant enabling Pakistan to produce in one year enough plutonium to produce 10 to 15 Nagasaki-sized bombs. Kissinger warned the Pakistani premier that he might jeopardize his position as a prime minister unless he curtailed his nuclear efforts. Kissinger also pressed the French premier Jacques Chirac to cancel the deal. There are signs that, because of this pressure, both Bhutto and Chirac lost their positions. The French reprocessing plant was built in Pakistan in 1975. But because of American pressure, the French insisted that Pakistan must only use Caramel – a low-grade uranium – rather than enriched uranium, which by itself is capable of being used to produce the bomb.

Pakistan was well aware of the difficulties it faced in the nuclear field. The Americans almost succeeded in blocking them from obtaining plutonium needed for the bomb. Pakistan therefore decided to choose another alternative: to enrich uranium in its own plants. Hundreds of Pakistani students were sent to France, Italy, Germany and Holland in order to learn these special techniques. One of them, Abdul Kamar Gun, worked for two years at the Dutch nuclear centre in Almado, controlled by Great Britain, West Germany and Holland. In 1975 the engineer disappeared. Top-secret plans for building an ultra-modern centrifuge for enriching uranium disappeared with him.

In 1981 the Pakistani nuclear programme, Project 706, was way ahead of that of any Arab state. Intelligence agencies all over the world estimated that the Pakistanis might have reached already the 'bomb-in-the-basement' stage and that they were likely to test one of their nuclear devices soon. These estimates proved to be wrong. Two decades would pass before Pakistan would publicly expose its nuclear arsenal and the Indian subcontinent would openly reach the stage of a balance of nuclear terror.

Since Pakistan took no active part in any of the Middle East wars, Israel was not worried about a direct nuclear threat from this state: its main fears were over the collaboration between Pakistan, Libya and Iraq. Gaddafi was trying to achieve a ready-made bomb from the shelf, for the millions of dollars he had invested in this programme. For the Iraqis the story is different. They had their own nuclear plant – though they probably needed technical help from Pakistan – and by June 1981 they were ahead of all other Arab countries in the race to develop the bomb.

5

A Bomb in the Basement: Dayan's Formula

1963

Ben Gurion's successor as Prime Minister and Minister of Defence was Levi Eshkol. Coming from the position of Finance Minister, Eshkol was well aware of the financial details of the Israeli nuclear project, but he was not a professional military man, and there were two people with whom he was to work very closely on the problem: Yitzhak Rabin – the Chief of Staff of the Israeli Army – and Yigal Allon, the dynamic Minister of Labour. Both Rabin and Allon were former members of the Palmach – the special SNS (Special Night Squad) forces of the Jewish Haganah. They both believed in adopting only conventional strategy for Israel, they were against the nuclear doctrine espoused by Ben Gurion in his last years in power, and they demanded the allocation of more money towards the conventional army.

In the political field, Israel agreed to American inspection visits and some American control of its nuclear plants in Dimona and Nahal Sorek. US President Lyndon Johnson agreed in return to supply Israel with American weapons, among them the Skyhawk A-4-E fighter bombers, and M-48 Paton tanks, and other modern weapon systems.

Ben Gurion had been against this type of policy – a trade-off between the Israeli independent nuclear option for conventional arms. One of the main topics of the 1965 election campaign was Ben Gurion's accusation against Levi Eshkol of a 'big mishap' and a small one. By the 'big mishap' Ben Gurion meant Eshkol's surrender to American pressures over the nuclear reactor in Dimona.

But Eshkol did not stop the Israeli efforts. What he actually did was to opt for a short-term nuclear option, but no more than that. This meant in effect that if any dramatic changes were to have happened in the Middle East, Israel could use its potential quite quickly. It was Eshkol who said, 'Israel would not be the first to introduce nuclear weapons in the Middle East but neither would it be the second in the race.' This seems to have become the Israeli official nuclear policy since that time.

This policy of nuclear abstention in exchange for US support (in terms of conventional arms and economic aid) continued until the end of the 1960s. But the internal crisis before the beginning of the 1967 war reopened the nuclear policy debate. In June 1967, trying to gain national support, Eshkol called on Dayan to serve as Minister of Defence. The right-wing party, the Gahal bloc, headed by Menachem Begin, joined the new coalition as well and a national unity government was established. The return of Dayan to the government as Minister of Defence raised the question of Israeli nuclear doctrine. Dayan was confronted by Allon, who claimed Israel should continue its conventional doctrine. An Israeli nuclear bomb, Allon said, would mean a new nuclear arms race in the Middle East. According to him, Israel's vulnerability to nuclear attacks, because of its inferiority in terms of territory and population, would make for an intolerable situation. This, and the fact that Arab rulers could be both unreliable and irrational, added to his fear of nuclear Armageddon.

Eskhol, who was not an expert in military and strategic affairs, preferred not to have to decide whether or not Israel should go to the final stage of reaching a 'bomb in the basement'. According to some researchers, this decision might have been adopted by Dayan, who served as Minister of Defence in the cabinet of an old woman still haunted by nightmares of pogroms in Czarist Russia: Golda Meir.

The newly appointed Israeli premier came to power after the death of Eshkol in February 1969. In the past Golda Meir had objected to the nuclear doctrine suggested by Ben Gurion, Peres and Dayan. Ben Gurion, the old leader, had ceased his political activities by the end of 1960. But both Peres and Dayan were members of Mrs Meir's cabinet. Dayan was the one who developed a new formula, that of 'a bomb in the basement'.

Experience of the 1967 war proved to the Minister of Defence that Israel was dependent for its security on foreign powers. The French embargo on conventional arms to Israel immediately after the war, the refusal of the British government to sell Chieftain tanks to Israel and the conditions that the USA gave Israel while selling it arms proved to be too risky from Dayan's point of view. According to his logic, Israel could independently achieve most of the means to secure its future. Thus, in Dayan's days at the Defence Ministry the decision was reached to build independent Israeli weapon systems, such as the Kfir (a fighter bomber) and the new Israeli main battle tank, the Merkava.

Such means as these could secure the Jewish state's future, as long as only the Arabs were involved in the conflict. But Dayan was mainly worried about the Soviet Union. Since Russian support for the Arabs had been guaranteed for many long years, while the same could hardly be said about US relations with Israel, Israel's diplomatic capabilities were limited in advance. In order to improve this capability, to secure those territories that it believed necessary for its defence, Israel had to create uncertainty over Russian readiness to become directly involved in the conflict. Israel needed to deter the USSR.

The war of attrition along the Suez Canal, the acts of Palestinian terrorism within the Israeli borders and abroad, as well as preparations made by other Arab armies for a war against Israel, all contributed to Dayan's fears. But more than anything else Dayan was frightened by the possibility that in the long run Israel would not be able to afford in economic terms a new conventional arms race in the Middle East. Although Israel's victory in 1967 was absolute the Arabs did not show any sign that they were ready to enter negotiations: in fighting the wars of attrition along its borders Israel faced grave economic difficulties, and maintaining a strong conventional army became a very great burden on the Jewish state.

In order to get out of this dead end, Dayan developed a new formula that would help Israel to keep the territories it needed for its defence, as well as to bear the increasing costs of a conventional army. The formula stated that: diminishing the intensity of the conflict (by giving back some territories to Egypt and Syria), plus a credible Israeli deterrent, plus an adequate conventional army to maintain self-defence and small-scale wars, equals reasonable security at a reasonable price.

According to this doctrine Israel would be able to return some of the occupied territories and limit its military budget. Giving back part of the territories would diminish Arab motivation to go to war and this motivation would diminish even more when the Arabs found out about the Israeli nuclear option.

This logic of Dayan's is still valid even today. But in order to implement it, Israel must both return all the territories occupied in 1967 and give publicity to the fact (at least assumed by all experts in this field) that it has a nuclear option.

The flaw of this strategy is that, once chosen, it cannot be reversed. The official policy is to demand a nuclear-free zone in the Middle East, similar to agreements signed by Latin American states. Dayan, while serving as Foreign Minister, stated in the United Nations that all Israel's Arab neighbours should 'join it in direct negotiations with a view to establishing a nuclear-free zone in the Middle East'.

Israel's Ambassador to the UN, Professor Yehuda Bloom, said on 27 November 1978, 'The government of Israel has stated on several occasions that it would not be the first to introduce nuclear weapons into the Middle East. That is an official government statement. It is an official undertaking of which responsible quarters the world over have duly taken note.' (While understanding this Israeli declaration one must take into consideration the way the Israelis then saw the UN. They considered it to be an impotent organization and therefore they used it only as a platform for propaganda.)

At the beginning of the 1970s Dayan made various declarations concerning Israel's nuclear capability. On the other hand, he assured the world that no Arab state would go to war with Israel until the end of that decade. Taking into consideration that the development of a nuclear option would take at least 8–10 years, it is clear why Dayan was so confident of Israel's superiority over the Arabs.

But Dayan was to find out sooner than he had imagined that the mind of Egypt's new president was rather different.

The October war surprised Israel. The IDF estimated that Egypt and Syria would not go into full-scale war with Israel unless they were capable of neutralizing the Israeli Air Force and were able to penetrate with low-altitude fighter bombers into the heart of the country. This concept took account of only some elements of the Arabic capability, and therefore it does not make much sense. We can also assume that the Israelis evaluated another element: their nuclear superiority. It was estimated in the military and civil intelligence centres that the Arabs would not declare a new war against Israel because it might lead to nuclear confrontation. When this element is taken into consideration, the Israeli conception makes much more sense. Of course, the Israelis never admitted that this was the basis for their conception on the eve of Yom Kippur, 1973, because this would mean that they held the bomb. But this is still the only way to understand the logic of their behaviour during that dramatic event.

The Israeli strategic view failed on two grounds. Firstly, the Egyptian and Syrian armies built a surface-to-air missile umbrella, thus neutralizing Israeli superiority in the air, and, secondly, the war aims were considered as limited from the beginning by Sadat and Assad. By planning a limited territorial war, Sadat and Assad hoped to mitigate Israel's atomic threat. They were sure that Israel would not operate nuclear weapons against them as long as they did not endanger the existence of the State of Israel within the 1967 borders.

The first stages of the war were better than even the most optimistic Egyptian and Syrian generals could have planned. The Egyptian Army succeeded in occupying the 'Bar Lev' line that was defended by a small force of tanks and infantry troops. They were able to occupy a strip five miles wide all along the Suez Canal. In the north, Syrian tank divisions succeeded in cutting through the Israeli lines and were nearly occupying the whole of the Golan Heights. According to the different reliable sources, Defence Minister Dayan regarded the situation of 8 October 1973 as critical to Israel's security and existence. In Golda Meir's office he offered his resignation because of what he saw as his part in the responsibility of the Israeli failure. 'We are going to lose the Third Temple', he warned Mrs Meir.

Against this apocalyptic background, it seems that a decision to consider the use of a nuclear threat was made by Israel's top establishment officials. There are indications that Dayan gave an order secretly to put in combat readiness, for the first time, Israeli-made Jericho SS missiles, carrying nuclear warheads, as well as Kfir and Phantom bomber fighters equipped with nuclear devices. Altogether, 13 Israeli-made nuclear weapons were put on alert. If this was so, it was the first time Israel had fulfilled its nuclear option. Of course, Israeli sources denied any rumour concerning this particular atomic alert. If this was a fact, it is hard to say what Dayan's intention was in giving this order. It might be possible that he considered launching the missiles as a realistic option. But it is more reasonable to consider it as a clear signal to both the USA and the USSR. Dayan could be sure that the superpowers, who had special reconnaissance satellites over the Middle East, would immediately monitor Israeli activity and understand its significance. To the USSR it would come as a warning not to take part directly in the war. The USA was supposed to understand that Israel, under severe pressure, was in such a condition that it might use its last-resort capability and bring a nuclear Armageddon to the Middle East. Only a massive shipment of conventional weapons, to change the situation in the battlefields, would convince the Israeli leadership not to opt for its nuclear capability.

In order to achieve that, the USA had to airlift arms to Israel. There were many delays in sending the arms, in spite of Israeli pressures. The Israeli signals would make it clear to the decision-makers in the White House, the Pentagon and the State Department that any more delays might bring catastrophe to the Middle East. As for the Russians, Dayan realized that they would supply their clients, Egypt and Syria, with the necessary information about this particular Israeli move. If this happened, Dayan was sure that both Sadat and Assad would limit their war aims, in order to avoid an Israeli nuclear response.

The Israeli signals seem to have gained some results; the Americans started supplying the IDF with growing quantities of US-made conventional arms by airlift. The Arab armies did limit their aims, and, in any event, were blocked by the winning Israeli forces.

The USSR had sent, either as a reaction, or as a means to support possible direct Soviet involvement in the war, a ship loaded with nuclear devices to the Egyptian port of Alexandria. While crossing the Dardanelle straits the Americans found out what it contained by using sensitive sensors. The meaning of this Russian move was not absolutely clear either to the Americans or to the Israelis. But at a post-mortem they were able to conclude two things: firstly, as a blackmail measure against the Americans the nuclear option had proved to be very efficient. On this score further credence could be given to a pro-independent Israeli nuclear doctrine that would increase Israel's freedom of action. The second conclusion, mainly maintained by those who were against a policy of a 'bomb in the basement', argued that Israel's latent threat to destroy Arab countries if they declared a war against it and endangered its existence, had not proved successful because in such conditions Sadat had preferred to ignore the latent threat, and both Egypt and Syria had achieved nuclear guarantees from the USSR to neutralize the possible Israeli nuclear threat.

But it seems that the Israeli nuclear threat had one effect that was still hidden and little understood back in 1973. One of the main factors which changed Sadat's policy toward peace with Israel was his belief in the Israeli bomb.

The 'Yom Kippur' War created an internal crisis in Israel. Although the final results of the war were relatively satisfactory, the way the war started, the surprise, and the failure of the military's plan, created a political earthquake across the country. Golda Meir had to resign under the pressure of public criticism. Dayan left the cabinet with her. Yitzhak Rabin, the Chief of Staff of the winning Israeli Army in 1967, was appointed Prime Minister and Shimon Peres became Minister of Defence.

One again, at the core of the Israeli cabinet stood two persons who were divided on the problem of Israel's nuclear doctrine. But this time the problem seemed to be different. Since Israel was considered to have had the bomb from the beginning of the 1970s, two main topics were left for the debate between Rabin and Peres: (1) How far should Israel continue in developing its nuclear potential in relation to the conventional one? (2) Should Israel declare its nuclear doctrine openly, mainly as a measure to deter Arab aggressiveness?

Shimon Peres, one of the top architects of Israeli's nuclear capability, believed for many years that only nuclear potential could bring peace. He considered this could be done in two phases:

> The great danger about missiles (and anything that is said about missiles is true about other similar weapon systems) is in the case that only the aggressive side, i.e. the Arabs, would have them. On the other hand, in the case that both sides should have this capability, it may limit not only the will of aggressiveness, but also the danger of war ... because the truth is that both sides are vulnerable enough not to play with military plans.
>
> (*The Next Phase* (1965) p. 179)

According to Peres this was the first phase; the creation of a balance of terror in the Middle East. Israel would never be able to reach it without declaring publicly its nuclear doctrine and without developing its nuclear option.

According to Peres, when the Middle East reached this stage, the next one would come:

> Peace will not come by itself ... it will not be brought by outside foreign nations ... it will not grow on the present political background of the Middle East, but Israel can bring it closer if she convinces the Arabs that by using science they will have no chance to hit us, not only in the present but also in the future.
>
> (Ibid.)

Peres almost always uses innuendo and euphemisms in his articles. When he speaks about 'science' one can assume he means mainly Israel's trump card – nuclear technology. From the new Defence Minister's point of view, this weapon was the main political argument which could make it clear to the Arabs that they would never be able to destroy Israel without destroying themselves, and therefore they must make peace with it.

Against this pro-nuclear strategist stood Rabin who, since

the beginning of the 1960s had been preparing the Israeli Army for conventional warfare. Between 1968 and 1973 Rabin served as Israeli Ambassador to the USA, and in Washington he developed a new concept, according to which Israel's security was more dependent on decisions made in the White House than upon decisions taken in government offices in Jerusalem. Since for the previous twenty years the USA had strongly opposed efforts by any state to acquire an independent nuclear device, and since it was clear to Rabin that an independent open Israeli nuclear doctrine would harm the American–Israeli relationship, he opposed the strategy suggested by Peres. While Prime Minister, Rabin demanded special relations with the US, even getting approval from the US before making any Israeli diplomatic initiative, Peres pressed for nuclear and open strategy, thus harming the Israeli–US relationship.

Rabin's policy, therefore, was to use the Israeli nuclear option as a lever to gain economic, diplomatic and military aid from the US. He saw the nuclear trump card as a measure to get peace or at least a non-belligerent status with the Arab states. Against the background of these different points of view many clashes occurred between the Premier and his Minister of Defence. One example typifies this.

In June 1974 President Nixon paid a visit to the Middle East. During his visit a deal was offered between the US and Egypt and the US and Israel. According to this deal each of these two Middle Eastern states was to receive two nuclear-powered electricity stations. For Israel, which is almost totally dependent on external sources for its energy, the deal was very important, as it was for the Egyptians. In August 1976, the negotiations ended in Washington and agreements were signed initially between Egypt and the US, and Israel and the US. Although at one point the Americans under Carter were ready to approve the deal without any inspection, it became clear to all sides that ratification of the deal depended upon agreements by both Egypt and Israel to American inspections of their nuclear plants. The deal was due to be ratified by the middle of 1977, but then Rabin had to resign because of personal and domestic political problems and Peres became the new party leader till the elections of May 1977. This was followed immediately by a change in Israel's attitude the deal. Since Peres did not agree to the terms of the contract, especially those that dealt with the American inspection, the contract was never signed. Because of that the US to this day has no control over Israel's nuclear plants.

The debate between Rabin and Peres did not stop Israeli nuclear research. Already in 1972 Israeli scientists Isaiah Nebenzahl and Menachem Levin had reached a breakthrough in the enrichment process by using laser beams. In this new system, seven grams of U235 can be enriched to a degree of 60 per cent within one day. It is estimated by experts in this field that 50kg of 60 per cent enriched uranium are needed to build one bomb. In the 1980s, this was the cheapest of all processes known to exist to enrich uranium.

But this was not the only direction in which Israel was working. It seems that since the beginning of the 1970s, its goals have been to widen its nuclear arsenal, in quantity as well as quality, and in the field of launching systems. For this purpose Israel co-operated with both South Africa and Taiwan.

In September 1979, American and Soviet spy satellites detected a nuclear explosion over the Indian Ocean at a height of 26,000ft. The CIA and other intelligence services in the West estimated that it was a nuclear shell launched from a special 155mm cannon that was built by an American company called Space Research. This special cannon was purchased by Israel and the Republic of South Africa (RSA), which succeeded in by-passing American, British and Canadian control systems. Western intelligence sources estimated that the explosion in September 1979 was a joint experiment by the RSA and Israel in one of the most advanced tactical nuclear systems then known to be used anywhere in the world.

According to press reports in the late 1980s, Israel and the RSA even agreed to co-operate with a third nation. Taiwan (a state that feels it is under siege, especially since the USA improved its relations with Red China) has probably joined the not so exclusive club of pariah states. In the framework of this triple-state co-operation there are indications that a common effort was made to develop a cruise missile with a 1,500-mile range. Such a missile launched from Israel could hit any target within the Arab world, while also covering many targets in southern Russia. This type of missile can be launched from an airplane or a ship, thus increasing its range by many more miles. There were also signs that Israel and the RSA were managing to develop a neutron bomb; and that they were working on the tactical arsenal no less than one the strategic one.

Israel's position in the nuclear field is not (and probably never will be) absolutely clear, but it can be estimated that the effort that Ben Gurion started at the end of the 1950s has proven to be very fruitful from the Israeli nuclear strategists' point of view.

Although there are different appreciations of Israel's nuclear capabilities, CIA reports estimated that the number of operational nuclear warheads it owned in 1980 was around 200. Large numbers of these were for tactical purposes, with a destruction power of less than 20 kilotons. In the early 1980s Israel already had a variety of launching systems. The Phantom F-4E, the Israeli-made Kfir C2, or the F-15 and the F-16 were all fighters capable of delivering the bomb. Besides these Israel had, according to Western sources, at least three types of surface-to-surface missile capable of carrying a nuclear warhead. There were two types of the Israeli-French-made Jericho: the MD660 with a range of 450km; and the MD620 with a longer range and better navigation system. Israel also had the American-made Lance SS missile that was supplied after the Yom Kippur War. Its range was about 110km, but American experts believed that it could carry a tactical nuclear 11kg warhead of 1 kiloton to a range of 118km. By using inertial navigation systems it was very accurate and could hit a target within a range of 70km with a CEP (Circular Error Probability) of 100 metres.

Besides these launching systems, in the early 1980s Israel was estimated to be capable of obtaining at least two other systems by the end of the decade. One of them was a nuclear 'gun' and the other was the Cruise missile. It is unclear whether Israel ever obtained these two systems. But, in any event, the modern means by which it could launch nuclear weapons, already seemed to provide Israel, by the early 1980s, with a second-strike capability – a very important element for a state with a limited territorial space and manpower resources. Israel's improved strategic posture during the 1990s, especially after 'Desert Storm' and the collapse of the Soviet Union, did not

pave the way, however, to a radical change in its nuclear doctrine. Nevertheless, at the height of the Arab–Israeli peace
process in the mid-1990s, some Israeli officials hinted that in a
'new Middle East' Israel might give up its nuclear card. One
will have to wait until the 'new Middle East' is born, in order
to see whether the Israelis will, indeed, take such a drastic step.

6

Saddam Hussein and Project Tammuz

Iraq's acquisition of nuclear technology was the first Arab attempt towards nuclear arming, although the officially declared purpose of the construction of the reactor was not nuclear weapons.

Saddam Hussein in *Al Usbu Al-Arabi*
(Lebanon, 8 September 1975)

'Saddam rules the people with a gun in one hand and money in the other', Richard Lindley summed up in *The Listener*. Hussein, as president of the Revolutionary Command Council and secretary general of Ba'ath, is referred to by critics as 'the Butcher of Baghdad'. The Ba'athist officer who came to power in 1979 has maintained power through violence (in the tradition of recent political history) in a country where minority Sunni rulers have dominated a majority population of Shiites and Kurds since 1968. (In the late 1970s, Iraq's population was 29 per cent Sunni, 46 per cent Shiite, and 13 per cent Kurdish; by contrast, the Ba'athist-dominated Iraqi Army was 80 per cent Sunni, 14 per cent Shiite and 4 per cent Kurdish; Iraq's officer corps was 90 per cent Sunni.)

With an eye on the history of past successful dictatorships and tyrannies, Hussein, as head of the security forces and director of intelligence, had purged the army and executed or exiled a number of opposition Ba'athist, Shiite, and Kurdish officers. He had also created an elite party militia, or 'Regular Army', its members recruited from loyal party militants.

In 1978, the Iraqi regime grew even more violent and nepotistic. Hussein found the perfect instrument of terror in

Khairallah Hussein, his son-in-law and first cousin to Al-Bakr, the nominal ruler. Khairallah, Iraq's minister of defence since 1977 as well as the governor of Baghdad, organized a group of his own personal assassins and began a series of murders, including the 1978 shooting of former Iraqi prime minister Al-Naif in front of the Hilton Hotel in London. In 1979, Al-Bakr, ageing and perhaps not a little nervous, relinquished power to Hussein, who assumed the presidency of the Revolutionary Council. Once again, Hussein, ever careful to protect his flanks, unleashed Khairallah on about a dozen opposition Shiite officers, all of whom were rounded up, tortured, and killed in a brutal day-long operation reminiscent of Hitler's Night of the Long Knives. Hussein himself, along with his bodyguard, over-saw the ruthless slayings of the opposition Shiite officers.

By 1980, there is no doubt that Iraq was a country with enormous military potential and capacity. It had 13 million people, a gross national product of $18 billion, and a defence budget of $3.5 billion yearly. Its army consisted of 190,000 men, organized into 12 divisions, of which four are armoured and two mechanized. In its arsenal were 2,200 tanks (of which 1,000 were high-level, Russian-manufactured T-62s), 1,700 pieces of artillery, and assorted missiles. It also had an air force of 30,000 with such equipment as 450 attack aircraft (more than, for instance, Great Britain's total fighter aircraft), of which 140 were high-quality MiG 23-Bs, Sukhois (7B, 20), and Tupolev 22s. The Iraqi Navy comprised 4,000 sailors, and included 12 torpedo boats, 14 anti-missile boats, and 19 others. Since 1973, Iraq's army had grown from six or seven divisions to 12, plus three airborne brigades. In this period, its tank force had doubled and its total of combat airplanes had increased from 250 to 450 while the number of helicopters jumped from 80 to 225. Iraq had also acquired a fleet of tank carriers that potentially could be used against Israel.

Last and most ominously, Iraq was the only Arab country in the Middle East to develop a nuclear capacity, which we will discuss later in this chapter.

Hussein and Iraq had two ambitions in the Gulf, one of a gener-al and long-term nature, the other immediate and territorial. Iraq wanted, and still wants, nothing less than to be the dominant

Arab power in the Persian Gulf, replacing a slowly disintegrating Iran, which in the late 1970s almost solely focused on its own internal politics and its hostility towards the United States. According to the Iraqi press, in 1980, Hussein was seeking to gain control over Iranian Khuzistan (or Arabistan, as termed by Iraq), and Iranian Baluchistan, and Kuwait, all of which, not coincidentally, are oil-rich. Iran and Iraq, in fact, fought a number of small wars between 1973 and 1975 over the area on either side of Shatt al Arab, the river border that separates Khuzistan from Iraq. The 1975 Algiers–Tehran agreement between the Shah and Hussein (in which Iran promised to stay out of Iraqi Kurdistan and Iraq promised to cease hostilities in Iranian Khuzistan) is no longer valid. In September 1980, the old war flared up again at precisely the moment that a beleaguered and divided Iran faced US sanctions and the rupture of formal diplomatic relations.

Hussein's complementary goal next to Gulf hegemony was the destruction of Israel. His anti-Israeli stance had been stringent, consistent and open at least since 1978, when, in a Baghdad radio speech, he declared that 'the essence of the Iraqi regime's stand on the Arab–Israeli conflict is principled and immovable on a total rejection of any political solution. Settlement lies in an all-out military struggle, aimed at uprooting Zionism from the area'.

A year before, Hussein and the then-nominal Iraqi ruler, Ahmed Hassan al-Bakr, along with President Hafez Assad of Syria, created the Charter of National Action, the foundation for the Rejectionist Front. The Front itself was created at a Tripoli meeting in December 1977 and comprised Iraq, Syria, Libya, Algeria, South Yemen and the Palestine Liberation Organization. In the wake of Sadat's trip to Jerusalem, the Front called for an economic war against Sadat, Zionism and American imperialism.

Since that time, the Front, headed by a militarily dominant Iraq, has been a powerful force in keeping moderate states such as Saudi Arabia and Jordan in line. Iraq has served as a sanctuary for the most radical Arab and Palestinian groups, including groups once directly connected with Moscow, such as the Abu Nidal (Black June) group operating in South Yemen. Iraq has also supported the Dhofar revolution in Oman.

Of all Arab nations Iraq is certainly the one nearest to acquiring the A-bomb, motivated by the desire to be the leader of the Persian Gulf, the Arab countries and the Third World. To make this policy operative, Iraq has been increasing its military power at an unprecedented rate, utilizing its petrodollars and seeking to develop a technological military infrastructure, with the result that during 1973–81 Iraq accumulated a strong conventional arsenal to become the strongest nation of all the Arab countries. But this was not enough for Hussein. Since the mid-1970s Iraq has been building up its power in yet one more field – the nuclear one.

Iraqi efforts can be traced back to the year 1959. It was then that the Iraqi government issued Rule No. 45 establishing the Iraqi Nuclear Energy Committee. In 1964 the premier appointed himself as the chairman of this committee. Today, Saddam Hussein serves in this capacity.

Iraq was accepted into the International Atomic Energy Agency (IAEA) in 1959. On 29 October 1969, it signed the Non-Proliferation Treaty and on 14 March 1972 ratified it, indicating that acceptance of it did not mean that Iraq recognized the state of Israel.

On 20 July 1960, Iraq signed an agreement with the USSR concerning the building of a research reactor. In 1963 the Soviets started building the project in Al Tawita, about 20km south-east of Baghdad. The project – IRT 2000 2MW thermal power reactor – was completed in 1968. Ten years later, the Soviets agreed to change the fuel of the reactor. Instead of 10 per cent enriched U235, it was operating now on 80 per cent enriched uranium and its power was raised to 5MW.

The Soviets supplied Iraq with other facilities, thus allowing them to build a whole nuclear complex in Al Tawita, which included a laboratory to produce radio isotopes, special physics laboratories and other small projects. About a hundred Iraqi students were sent to the USSR to complete their studies in nuclear physics.

This Soviet-made project, near Baghdad, was sufficient for a Third World country interested in modern technology. But for Iraq's Ba'athist regime it was not good enough. Russian technicians had been inspecting the reactor since 1968. With such close inspections the Iraqis realized that they would never have a chance to get enough military-grade uranium or plutonium to produce a bomb. If they wanted it, they would have to obtain help from other sources.

Due to Iraq's status as one of the biggest oil suppliers to the West, the Iraqi leaders came to the conclusion that they would have a good chance of acquiring the installations and nuclear know-how in western Europe. The Western states, particularly France and Italy, had two great advantages compared to the USSR from Iraq's point of view. First, they were ready to supply Iraq with the equipment needed to reach a nuclear option. Second, their nuclear technology was far more advanced than that of the Russians, especially in the field of manufacturing weapon-grade ore, i.e. enriched uranium and plutonium.

On 7 April 1975, a scientific conference was held in Baghdad. Besides Iraqi nuclear scientists, other Arab as well as American and west European scientists took part. We can assume that this event was a breakthrough in Iraqi efforts to produce the bomb. The first connections between the head of the Italian nuclear fuel department of CNEN (Italian Nuclear Energy Committee) and Iraqi scientists were forged. Thus the process that led to the Israeli raid on the Iraqi reactor had started.

By 1975 it was well known that the Shah of Iran, Iraq's neighbouring enemy, had embarked upon an ambitious nuclear programme that would enable him to acquire the bomb within less than a decade. But the Iraqis were not only motivated by fear of Iran. The leadership of the Ba'athist party had its own ambitions – to control the Persian Gulf and to be a leading state in the Third World. An A-bomb could be a definite measure to reach this prestigious and powerful position. The Iraqis therefore decided to accelerate their plans and the first country they turned to also proved to be the most reliable one: France.

In September 1975, Hussein, at that time Vice-President but already the strong man of the Iraqi regime, paid a visit to France. After long discussions a nuclear co-operation agreement between the two states was signed on 18 November 1975, however, even before signing this agreement, the Iraqis were interested in French nuclear technology which could be used for military as well as civil purposes. They asked the French to supply them with a 500-megawatt electricity-powered gas graphite reactor. This type of reactor had been built in France during 1959–72 and was used not only as a power station but also for plutonium production. Graphite reactors were also built in the USA and the UK, probably even in the USSR. Although they were operated as power stations, the superpowers used them mainly for plutonium production. By the end of the 1960s, better and much more efficient systems were found for electrogeneration. The Western states stopped producing this type of reactor and when Iraq demanded a gas graphite reactor, it could be understood only if one took into consideration the fact that this reactor produces 40kg of military-grade plutonium per annum.

The French rejected Saddam Hussein's request for a dual-purpose gas graphite reactor. Instead they offered the Iraqis another research programme and facilities which could only indirectly give them a nuclear option. This was the ultra-advanced Osiris research reactor with an extremely high thermal power compared with other research models, and operating on enriched uranium.

It is well known that materials change their properties as a result of extended irradiation. Therefore, it is necessary to study the results of radiation on the materials of a reactor's structure. The Osiris belongs to a group if reactors named 'Material Test Reactors' (MTR). This type of reactor is designed exactly for the above-mentioned purpose. No wonder, therefore, that such reactors are used only by great industrial powers in the field of development and production of power reactors. Since Iraqi industry is hardly one of the most developed in the world, and since there was no evidence that it was going to be a power reactor builder, Iraq's choice of the Osiris research reactor seems to have been absurd. But Osiris did have one quality which made it suitable for Iraqi purposes, although it never confirmed them. It was one of the best existing research reactors for the production of weapon-grade plutonium in substantial quantities.

The French, as well as the Americans, were of course aware of the implications of the Iraqi programme based on this type of reactor, and there were other clues as to Iraq's real goal.

On 15 January 1976, an agreement was signed between

Italy and Iraq, by which the Italians agreed to supply the Iraqis with the equipment and technical know-how of a vast field of nuclear problems, including the recycling of nuclear fuel and a particular system for reprocessing radiated nuclear fuel. This is in fact another name for plutonium separation.

By the end of 1976 the Iraqis were well ahead in fulfilling their nuclear ambitions. In the context of the agreement reached with France, the Osirak project, as it was now called, had started. Under the Osirak umbrella two types of reactors were built in 1977. The first was the 70MW Osiris; the second a small research nuclear reactor named Isis. The Iraqis then changed the name of the whole project to '17 Tammuz' (17 July), the date that the Ba'athist party came to power; the Osiris reactor was renamed Tammuz I, and the smaller reactor Tammuz II. Under the Tammuz project some special physics labs were also established (for further information on the structure and administration of the project and the names of the various reactors and systems, see Appendices 3 and 4). To control the quality of the project another French consortium was set up at the beginning of 1978.

While the French consortium was constructing the Tammuz project, another agreement was signed on 8 February 1978. This was a contract between the Italian CNEN as well as the Italian firms, SNIA Techint and AMN and the Iraqi government. The name of the new project was '30 July'.

For the Iraqis this was almost as important as the Tammuz project. Some other Italian firms were involved in it as subcontractors and it included the following facilities.

A Technological Hall for Chemical Engineering Research, described as a 'cold' facility for training in the cycling of spent fuels of a semi-industrial scale (i.e. 100–200kg of uranium per day). It contained most components of a 'hot' facility, as insisted by the Iraqis who claimed they wanted this lab to be as close to a plutonium separation plant as possible. Few changes were needed to undertake plutonium separation in this complex. The 30 July project also allowed the Iraqis the option of a MTR production line, which was the fuel used in the 'Tammuz I' reactor. In order to run in this facility, the Iraqi purchased from Italy 6 tons of low-grade uranium, 4 tons of natural uranium and 2 tons of 2.7 per cent enriched uranium.

A Technological Hall for Testing Materials was designed for research into nuclear structure and the effects of corrosion, including a thermo-hydraulic research centre. The '30 July' project included also a Radio Isotope Production Lab as well as 26 hot cells equipped for extensive production of radioisotopes.

Some 150–200 Iraqi scientists were sent to France to study advanced nuclear technology. Another 150 Iraqi engineers and technicians were sent for advanced studies in Italy. Saddam Hussein, who was personally in charge of the nuclear project on the site of Al Tawita, knew that diversion of adequate manpower resources was a key to success in operating such a massive nuclear programme. 'The strong man of Baghdad', as the foreign mass media were calling him, knew what the final goal of the whole project was to be. The Italians and the French, cynical and hypocritical as they were, would never enable him to produce the bomb while their technicians were still present at the Tammuz site. The Iraqis knew that they would have to send the foreigners away from Al Tawita before they could inaugurate the process needed to produce the bomb. Therefore, they had to prepare sufficient qualified personnel in advance to be able to run the project when all the foreign scientists and technicians had left.

Apart from the contracts and co-operation agreements that the Iraqis made with Italy and France, they looked forward to more co-operation with other states as well. Brazil was one of them, and on 8 January 1980, both countries reached an agreement according to which Brazil was to supply Iraq with uranium ore and low-grade enriched uranium. Brazilian scientists arrived in Baghdad in June 1980 to test the possibilities of mining uranium in Iraq itself. The Iraqis saw their agreement with Brazil as a very important one, since Brazil was supposed to be receiving the technology of uranium enrichment from West Germany. Iraq, in turn, expected to get this technology from Brazil, which would thus open up a new option for production of the bomb: the enriched uranium type.

The Iraqis were also trying to accumulate as much uranium as they could from all over the world. In 1980 they bought 120 tons from Portugal and 200 tons from Niger. In the future they also intend to buy uranium from Morocco. Western intelligence agencies estimated that Iraqi agents had tried to buy weapon-grade uranium from other states, but so far without success. In this sphere of activity they employed the services of arms dealers and some dubious parties in the Third World.

The negotiations between Iraq and Pakistan were as secret as they were significant. As we have already described, Pakistan had in the late 1970s the most advanced nuclear technology in the Muslim world. Although few details were not yet known, it was clear that agreements between these two states could be in such sensitive fields as uranium enrichment, plutonium separation and even the building of nuclear devices.

By mid-1980, Saddam Hussein, President of Iraq since the previous year, must have been highly satisfied with his country's advance towards nuclearisation.

The first 12kg of 93 per cent enriched uranium was shipped from France by the end of June 1980. Altogether Iraq was to receive from France about 80kg of this type of reactor fuel to operate its Tammuz I and Tammuz II reactors. If Iraq had chosen an instant approach to the bomb, it could have had 80kg of weapon-grade uranium – enough for 4–6 Hiroshima bombs. But this option was only good for an emergency situation. In the long run Saddam Hussein and his colleagues in the Ba'athist party could expect both projects – the French-made 17 Tammuz and the Italian-made 30 July – to be operating by the end of 1981. The combination of both could give them a plutonium cycle immediately. Now, top Iraqi nuclear scientists described to the 'strong man of Baghdad' how they were going to continue the project for producing the plutonium needed for the bomb after the foreign personnel had left.

In general, the only means of producing plutonium is by the irradiating of uranium targets in an appropriate reactor. The Iraqis had already acquired this type of reactor; the Osiris renamed Tammuz I. After that, the plutonium produced in these targets must be separated from the uranium and the fissionable materials, the radioactive waste, dealt with and the latter's disposal ensured.

The Iraqi scientists went on, describing to their leader how, with the facilities acquired from France, Italy and other states, they would be able to manufacture the bomb independently.

The Tammuz I reactor was an almost perfect duplicate of the French Osiris, but since no two reactors are one hundred per

45

cent identical, it was only an imperfect duplicate. It had two components: the main reactor (Tammuz I) – a light-water enriched uranium (93 per cent) open-core 70 megawatt thermal power reactor, fuelled by a 12kg U-235 load. Under conditions of continuous operation, the reactor would require three to four such fuel loads per annum. A second reactor (Tammuz II) was located in the vicinity of Tammuz I. This reactor was identical to Tammuz I in all details, except for the fact that it did not possess a cooling system, and hence could not be operated to capacity. Its fuel and load were identical to that of Tammuz I.

The Osirak reactors were designed for the irradiation of nuclear power station structure materials with a high neutron flow, in order to determine their resistance to such radiation. For this material test function Osirak was programmed to emit a high neutron flow (up to 4×10^{14} net/cm^2) and a large excess of radioactivity. The high flow enables high irradiation in a relatively short time period while the excess radiation enables the simultaneous irradiation of large quantities of structure materials. This excess radiation can likewise, however, be used for the irradiation of natural (or depleted) uranium in order to produce plutonium.

It is possible to produce significant quantities of plutonium in the Osirak reactor in the following way: all of the reactor's regular fuel and control elements are concentrated in the 5×5 central sites of the grid, while targets for irradiation (comprising natural or depleted uranium) are replaced in the remaining 31 sites. When the reactors are operated, in this configuration of 70MW power, 7–10kgs of plutonium may be produced per annum (according to the type of targets irradiated). In order to produce weapon-grade uranium in this manner, 10 tons of natural uranium are needed per annum.

The Iraqi nuclear scientists explained to Hussein that the substitution of a less highly enriched fuel – like the French-made 'Caramel' which was being offered because of American pressures n France – would not substantially alter the quantity of plutonium which could be produced in the Al Tawita project.

A number of essential auxiliary installations were also needed to produce the plutonium. All of the required auxiliary installations were designed and erected by well-known Italian and French companies. The increased capacity of the Iraqi installations could in the future enable Iraq to produce even more than 7–10kg of plutonium per annum.

Iraq acquired a semi-industrial installation for the production of PWR fuel from which uranium oxide pellets could be developed to manufacture suitable fuel for irradiation in the Osirak reactor. This installation, known as a fuel fabrication laboratory, can process 25 tons of uranium per annum. Although for the foreseeable future Iraq could have no possible use for the products of this installation, the scientists went on to explain that these products would also be irradiated in the reactor to produce plutonium. They reminded Hussein that Iraq had acquired hundreds of tons of uranium ores from Portugal, Niger and Italy. These acquisitions would ensure several years' supply of raw materials for the production installation.

The second phase, after the irradiation of the uranium and the production of plutonium, is the separation process. This is a chemical process in which large quantities of highly radioactive substances are dissolved and plutonium is extracted from uranium and fissile materials. To use plutonium for a second time it must be separated from the fissile materials and reprocessed separately. After plutonium is separated and transmitted into metallic form, it can then be turned into the form required for weapons, in small metallurgic installations contained in glove boxes.

In order to master the plutonium separation process, Iraq acquired a small 'hot lab' which permitted the separation of small quantities (several grams) of plutonium. This laboratory enabled Iraqi scientists and technicians to learn separation techniques and the handling of highly radioactive materials.

But Iraq was supplied by the Italians with a large-scale separation laboratory capable of separating uranium targets at the rate of 25 tons per annum. The problem with this installation was that it was designed without biological shielding, and some of the tanks contained in it could not withstand high irradiation. The Italians were not ready to supply Iraq directly with a separation plant which would allow the Iraqis to operate this separation process the minute they had enough materials to make it feasible. In order not to break the IAEA regulations, Italy supplied Iraq with an installation labelled as a 'demonstration' or 'training' facility to study the techniques of plutonium separation. But both Italian and Iraqi scientists knew that Iraq could overcome this obstacle in two different ways. Firstly, the biological shielding could be installed in the lab and a number of the tanks could be replaced, thereby converting this facility into a fully operative 'hot' facility. Secondly, the Iraqis were fully capable of making an exact copy of the facility with all the equipment needed for a 'hot' lab at another site.

The scientists concluded that though this was the most normal and regular way to reach the bomb, other channels were also open to them.

The first was the easiest from the technological point of view. As already noted, the fuel load of each Osirak reactor is 12kg of 93 per cent enriched uranium 235, which is fully weapon grade. Under normal work conditions the Tammuz I reactor requires approximately three such fuel loads each year, while for the Tammuz II reactor one such fuel load is sufficient for several years. Thus the fuel required for both reactors is approximately 50kg of enriched uranium per annum. This weapon-grade quantity is sufficient to produce at least two relatively simple U-235 bombs. The agreement signed between the Iraqi government and France mentioned a quantity of 80kg of this 93 per cent weapon-grade uranium sufficient to produce at least four U-235 bombs. This was the easiest way for the Iraqis to produce the fissionable materials needed for a U-235 bomb. But with the agreements they now had with Brazil, which were to supply the Iraqi nuclear project with the facilities and technologies information required for uranium enrichment, the Iraqi scientists knew that within another few years they might have a third route to produce the bomb.

All this took place in the summer of 1980. The Iraqi scientists promised Saddam Hussein that if nothing unexpected happened, Project 17 Tammuz could be well under way within less than a year.

Saddam Hussein sat peacefully, evaluating the plan that had now been introduced to him. He hoped for the completion of this project as quickly as possible, but taking into consideration the obstacles to his plan up to that time, and the mysterious ways of reactors themselves, he braced himself for more problems than his optimistic scientists were predicting.

PART TWO

THE DECISION IS MADE

7

The Writing on the Wall: Sabotage in France

Although in the summer of 1980 the Iraqis were ahead in their nuclear programmes, they had had to cope with many difficulties and delays since the project had begun in 1975. A combination of diplomatic pressure and mysterious cloak-and-dagger activity must have warned them that the road to the bomb would not be an easy one.

The basic agreement signed between Iraq and France concerning the setting up of the 17 Tammuz project had been attacked on three fronts.

First, there was internal dissension in France. Immediately after the signing of the deal, André Giraud, head of the French Nuclear Energy Committee, protested that it might allow Iraq to join the exclusive nuclear club. An official of the Quai d'Orsay also protested against the deal, claiming that it might lead to similar agreements with other Arab states including Libya. A nuclear Middle East, in which rulers like Gaddafi or Saddam Hussein held the bomb, could be as dangerous to France as to Israel.

In 1976 the French premier – Jacques Chirac – had his own view of the deal. He saw Iraq as the future leading Arab state and as France's most important oil supplier. Chirac was not naïve and could guess very well why Saddam Hussein was so keen on this extravagant project, but he had decided that, no matter what obstacles might arise, the deal must be completed for France's sake. He therefore threatened to sack André Giraud if he did not complete the deal along the lines laid down in the agreement. But although the French premier could ignore the view of professional officials, he could not ignore the American protest.

The USA and USSR were always considered to be the most reliable states as far as the Non-Proliferation Treaty was concerned. Both had very advanced technology in the nuclear field and both had tried their best to prevent nuclear proliferation. The US also had the power to influence French behaviour, since it supplied France with most of the enriched uranium needed for the operation of the Osiris-type reactors. It appears that the US administration threatened France with an embargo on American enriched uranium transferred to Iraq, but that the French found an effective way to overcome this obstacle: they decided to supply Iraq with the weapon-grade uranium from France's own military strategic stocks. French President Giscard d'Estaing took personal control over the subject of the French assistance to Iraq, in order to avoid any more pressure and delays in the project.

But there was still one more country which feared the Iraqi project and protested against the assistance the French were giving it. At the beginning of 1976, under instructions from Yigal Allon, Israeli Minister of Foreign Affairs, the Israeli ambassador to France Mordechai Gazit paid a visit to the Quai d'Orsay. For a long time of course the Israelis had been worried by the French–Iraqi negotiations and, now that the deal had been signed, Gazit demanded explanations from the French government. He also protested to the head of the Quai d'Orsay, but in vain.

On 17 September 1976 the deal was ratified by the parliaments of both states, and although some French members of parliament protested against French–Iraqi co-operation, which might lead to a nuclear option, Giscard d'Estaing and Chirac had no problems in getting the support of the majority of the French parliament.

In December 1976 another event occurred that showed how serious the Iraqis were in obtaining a nuclear option via the 17 Tammuz project. US Secretary of State Henry Kissinger – who was well aware of likely developments in the Third World, should west European states go on supplying second- and third-class states with nuclear facilities, thus increasing nuclear proliferation – pressed the Western powers to hold a meeting in London to discuss this subject. The conference, which was set up by the most advanced Western powers in this special field (including the UK, France, West Germany, Italy, Canada, Japan and the USA) agreed that tougher restrictions than those of the IAEA needed to be imposed against nuclear co-operation with Third World states. France was obliged to sign the general agreement and, as a result, it announced cancellation of the agreement to supply Pakistan with a plant to enrich uranium. But, strangely enough, France did not say a word concerning the Iraqi project and the Americans also kept quiet.

For almost a year and a half nothing changed. The Iraqis and French could be well satisfied. The Tammuz project (as well as the 30 July Italian project) was running smoothly. Construction Navalset Industrielles de la Méditérranée, the French company contracted to construct the two reactor cores, finished its job and on 9 April 1979 the reactor cores were about to be shipped from southern France to Iraq. They never left French soil.

On 4 April 1979 three tourists holding European passports arrived in Toulon, on the French Mediterranean coast. Two days later, on 6 April, four more tourists had arrived and joined their friends in one of the small hotels of the city. On that same night they left Toulon in two small trucks and headed toward La Seyne-sur-Mer near the Côte d'Azur. In the big CNIM-consortium-owned hangar in the city's port, the two cores of Tammuz I and Tammuz II were ready to be shipped within 48 hours to Iraq. Security there was not the best in the world...

The seven-strong team had no difficulty entering the hangar and locating the two Iraqi reactor cores. Although fantastic stories later appeared in the popular press describing how the group were trying to steal elements from the core, this proved to be a complete fiction. They completed their sole mission perfectly. Military explosives had been attached to the Iraqi cores. The five men doing the job joined the other two waiting outside covering them. The seven went back to their trucks and within a few minutes had left the small town whose citizens were still asleep. At 3.00am a deafening explosion was heard in the port. A few minutes later another two explosions were heard.

Police, DST (the French security service) and military experts rushed to the hangar where they found the residue of the two technically perfect cores – a heap of crushed materials. Only an expert could have identified them as the original two reactor cores. The police also found in the hangar three other loads that had not exploded. Except for the reactor cores no other equipment in the big hangar had been damaged.

The identity and nationality of the combat team who had performed this ruthlessly professional job in La Seyne-sur-Mer have never been discovered. Whatever the conjectures, it is clear that there were many foreign powers who viewed the Iraqi project as a threat.

Immediately after the secret raid *Le Monde* and other key French newspapers received anonymous calls identifying themselves as members of an organization called 'the French Ecological Group', claiming to have destroyed the Iraqi equipment 'in order to neutralize dangerous weapons for the sake of the future of the human race'. No-one has heard of such a group before or since and the French security services had no doubt that no ecological group could carry out such a complicated and professional operation. The French DST therefore suspect other organizations: the most likely – and the most professional according to French media – was of course Mossad.

The Israeli secret service has achieved a remarkable reputation in its brief existence. Among other activities it carried out an operation at the beginning of the 1960s to disrupt Nasser's efforts to acquire surface-to-surface (SS) missiles with unconventional warheads. The French had no doubt that Israel had a direct interest in slowing down the Iraqi project or even stopping it. They had no doubt either, that Mossad would have been well able to carry out the mission. The media speculated that the raid could have been performed by the Israelis, but with inside help. There were hints that scientists from the French Nuclear Energy Agency supplied the Israelis with the information to carry out the job. If one takes into consideration that some of these scientists were well aware of what the Iraqi aims were, and were very worried about it too, this obviously makes sense. The Israelis also have a history of relations with France. Even after the official change of policy of France toward Israel, such contacts may still exist.

The *International Herald Tribune* went even further, hinting that the raid had been carried out by French secret service officials in the French government who understood at last that the deal with Iraq might endanger other states in the Middle East and that this was against France's own interests. Blowing up the cores was one of the last steps that they could take to keep control of Iraqi activity without harming French–Iraqi relations.

But other states and organizations were being linked with the raid. *Le Point* suggested that the CIA staged it to avoid nuclear proliferation in a very strategic part of the world. Libya's Colonel Gaddafi was another suspect. According to this version PLO terrorists undertook the raid for Gaddafi, who paid them handsomely. Russians, Syrians, even the Iraqis themselves were in one way or another suspect. And according to *Stern* a source from Mossad had revealed full details of the raid. Some of these details proved completely false.

The most probable assumption is that Israelis carried out the raid. They had the expertise, the ability to perform it, and, more than anything else, the motive, although this does not eliminate the possibility that they were given co-operation, mainly intelligence information.

The media's wild guesses demonstrated one very important fact. Apart from Israel, there were many other nations in the Middle East and all over the world who had reason to be frightened by the Iraqi project. For the Iraqis it was the writing on the wall. They preferred to ignore it but in just over a year another omen was to come.

Yahya El Meshad was a 50-year-old Egyptian-born scientist. He had a good academic background, with diplomas from both American and Russian universities. Colleagues considered him a first-class scientist in his field. During the 1960s he taught at the University of Alexandria in Egypt and worked as a scientist at the Egyptian Nuclear Research Centre in Einshas.

It seems that Egypt, who throughout the 1960s and 1970s had renounced the nuclear option, was too small for the quiet, ambitious scientist. When the Iraqi government began its nuclear project a new position was suggested for El Meshad. The Iraqi offer was good from the Egyptian scientist's point of view. The Iraqis had both the capability and the will to carry out a nuclear project and the money they paid was an added incentive. El Meshad was appointed to a senior position in the

Tammuz project. In the summer of 1980 he went to France, arriving there on 6 June with instructions from the Iraqi government to check that equipment and materials soon to be delivered to Baghdad were according to professional standards. There was one highly important item in this shipment: the first 12kg load of 93 per cent enriched uranium, which would bring the Iraqis close to an immediate nuclear option. The Egyptian scientist spent more than a week in France, mainly at the French Nuclear Centre in Fontenay-Aux-Rares but also in Saclay, Cadarache and Pierrelatte. On Friday, 13 June he had returned to the Hotel Meridien in Paris after shopping for his family back home. A 'please do not disturb' sign was on the door of his room No. 9041 throughout that Friday night.

The young chambermaid who came to clean the room on Saturday morning did not know whether to disturb the guest. After hesitating for a few minutes, she decided to open the door.

The scene could have been out of any B-movie. The body of the Egyptian scientist deposited between the two beds in the room; the carpet soaked with his blood; his body battered to death; his head a pulp.

The police found the body on Saturday morning but a curtain of secrecy shrouded the murder. Only on Thursday, 17 June, were the French press allowed to report the mysterious crime. This of course had everything to do with the identity of the murdered Egyptian. It seems that the French government contacted the Iraqis before releasing the story.

The murder of El Meshad was directly connected with the Iraqi nuclear operation. He worked for the Tammuz project and was one of their most highly trained scientists, possibly the best Arab scientist the Iraqis ever had.

The police soon found out about the special ambience of the hotel in which El Meshad had stayed. Attractive young women were known to offer their special services to the guests. One of them was 32-year-old Marie-Claude Magal, who gave El Meshad a 'friendly' suggestion on the evening he was murdered. Mlle Magal claimed that she had met the scientist at the entrance to the hotel and had accompanied him to his room, which he entered after rejecting her offer. She waited for some minutes in the corridor, hoping that he would change his mind, but in vain. While still waiting, she could hear voices in his room, but no signs of a fight, and no shouting.

The young prostitute told her story to the DST on 1 July 1980, who let her go only to regret it. When they wanted to call her for another interrogation they found she had been killed in a hit-and-run accident on 12 July.

Again, as with the raid on the reactor cores fourteen months earlier, the French security service could not trace the perpetrators of El Meshad's death. They could not even decide on the motive for the murder – romantic, sexual, criminal or political. The fact that El Meshad's wallet was left in his pocket with 1,400 francs in it led the investigators to exclude robbery as the motive. On the other hand, he was murdered so brutally that it did not seem to be the work of a professional agent. As with the reactor-core raid, the police could only guess what had happened. They deduced that a man had entered El Meshad's room while he was out. It could have been that the young prostitute was supposed to seduce him and keep him out of his room. Whatever the case, this failed and the scientist entered his room. The surprised man who was checking his papers (and probably his diary as well) had no other choice but to murder him. According to this version, El Meshad was not murdered, his death was an accident.

But there is another version, according to which the agent or agents had indeed planned to murder El Meshad. It was to be an example for all those scientists who were taking part in the Iraqi project. The brutal warning did frighten some French and Italian scientists but the Iraqis could overcome that problem. In spite of the different versions of the story and the fact that the French secret service could not trace the murderers, they were sure of one thing: that the young French woman had been murdered and whoever had done that was also responsible for El Meshad's death.

Again Mossad was linked to the case. But French secret service sources believed it was an amateur piece of work. Mossad was too professional to have done such a dirty job, and the Israelis themselves denied categorically that they were responsible for this act.

A short time after the murder Egyptian sources announced that Syrian agents working for the Soviets had committed the crime. According to these sources, the Russians needed to know what stage of development the Tammuz project had reached. The Syrians were supposed to photocopy the scientist's papers but he caught them in the act. They murdered him and left the hotel.

As was the case with the raid near Toulon, the welter of speculation proved one vital point: that the Iraqi project had many enemies. Many governments would have been only too happy to see if fail and some of them might even have acted in accordance with this ambition. But once again the Iraqis seem to have ignored the signs.

8

The Writing on the Wall: Tearing the Thread

Israel has a free press but it is well known that, like the press in any other democratic country, it can be manoeuvred to focus on any subject the government demands. For many months the Israeli press had kept relatively quiet about the Iraqi project, although it was perhaps the most dangerous threat ever to the existence of the Jewish state. But suddenly, in the middle of July 1980, the entire Israeli press and television began discussing the Iraqi project and the co-operation between Iraq, France and Italy. Articles with such headlines as 'A nuclear Arab bomb: A *casus belli* for Israel?', 'Israel regards the French adventure [in Iraq] as introducing the Middle East to the age of the first nuclear strike', were a new phenomenon in the Israeli press.

The Israeli chief of staff, Rafael Eitan, is known to be a very quite and unassuming person. In an interview on Israeli television, he was asked what he thought about Iraqi efforts concerning the bomb. For a notably taciturn person he gave a long answer:

> If the Iraqis get the bomb, it will be as though all the countries in this region are hanging from a light sewing thread, high above. Any attempt to use the nuclear bomb will lead immediately to the tearing of that thread and the crashing of the states.

His interviewer was clever enough not to ask him what he meant by this. But Eitan's answer was cleverly ambiguous. If Iraq did produce the bomb, then the whole of the Middle East would become hostage to it. Any attempt by the Iraqis to operate the bomb against Israel would lead to a Middle East Armageddon. This was probably a hint for the other Middle East states. Eitan's warning was supposed to signal to the other Arab states of the Middle East that it was in their interest, as it was in Israel's, for Iraq never to acquire the bomb.

But Eitan's answer could have another meaning too. Israel would never let a fanatic ruler like Saddam Hussein have the bomb, for its own existence would then be dependent upon his unexpected and crazy behaviour.

Other Israeli officials were even more explicit as to how they saw the Israeli reaction to the Iraqi nuclear project in the future. 'Israel cannot allow itself to sit and wait until an Iraqi atomic bomb falls on our heads', said Mattitiahu Shmulevitch, a top aide to Prime Minister Begin.

Another senior official, who asked not to be identified, hinted that, even more than Israel, other Arab states in the Middle East should be anxious about the Iraqi project. 'If anybody in the world is likely to use the bomb, it's Iraq', he said. 'First Iraq gets the bomb, then the Russians give nuclear weapons to Syria because they are scared to death by Iraq. Then Iran gets them and you have three of the most unstable maniacal regimes in the world with nuclear weapons.'

This concerned mainly the interests of the West, which is dependent on Middle Eastern oil. A nuclear war in this part of the world might lead to a destruction of oil sources in Iraq and Iran, but Saudi Arabia and the rest of the Persian Gulf kingdoms could also be involved, which could jeopardize a large part of the Middle Eastern oil reserves. It was in the interests of the Western world, as well as in the interests of Israel, to avoid such a situation, the Israelis tried to explain. But the West had a short-sighted policy. France and Italy, as well as other European countries, were ready to do almost anything in order to have oil now. Iraq, as a big oil supplier to western Europe and Japan, could quite easily blackmail them and even acquire the bomb with their co-operation.

The public crusade in the Israeli press of July 1980 gave the signal to the foreign press to join the Israelis. Although Israel was not the most popular and sympathetic subject in the western European press, European editors and reporters did understand the importance of what was happening: there was a flood of stories and articles about the Iraqi project and the co-operation between Iraq and some western European states.

If the new press campaign carried out by the Israeli government had merely aroused world attention to this threat it would have been considered only a partial success. But the campaign was especially aimed at one country – Iraq.

In the many articles published both in Israel and in foreign papers one warning constantly recurred: the Iraqi project at Al Tawita was a matter of life and death, and Israel would do its best to prevent the spread of nuclear devices over the Arab world. From this point of view, in the summer of 1980 Israel gave a public declaration of intentions, although it was not an official one.

As *Time* magazine put it, Israel had given a silent warning that if it considered Iraq close to reaching the bomb, it might use a pre-emptive strike on Iraq's nuclear facility. This assumption was based on an interview given to the magazine by Shamir, the Israeli Minister of Foreign Affairs. 'The Iraqi nuclear reactor', he said, 'may ignite the conflict in this region and cancel the efforts to reach peace.' No clearer indication could be given as to how the Israelis saw the nuclear project in Iraq by the summer of 1980. But the Iraqis preferred to ignore even this signal. Soon they were to learn that the crusade against their efforts had moved back to the silent and cruel world of secret operations.

Mario Fiorelli was the general manager of the Italian SNIA Techint company. According to the contract signed by the Iraqis with CNEN and SNIA Techint the Italians agreed to construct within the 30 July project 'hot' and 'cold' labs which would in the future enable the Iraqis to build an independent separation plant. This was the target of the next mysterious agency working against the Iraqi project.

On the night of 7 August 1980, a small bomb exploded near the door of Fiorelli's flat in Via della Lungearetta in Rome. The damage was minimal and nobody was hurt. The owner of the flat was out of town.

At the same time, two other bombs exploded at 34 Via A. Bargoni, the offices of SNIA Techint. Here the damage was worse. The furniture, as well as the air-conditioning system, was damaged and the walls were covered with holes and explosion marks.

The Italian security service were able to trace the organization behind these explosions: a group called 'The Committee to Safeguard the Islamic Revolution' had admitted responsibility for these two acts. But since nobody had heard of this group either before or after the raid, the Italians were as much in the dark as ever. One thing they could be sure of: like the attack on the Iraqi reactor cores in April 1979 and the murder of El Meshad in June 1980, it was surely intended as a warning to the Iraqis. But this time the warning had a dual purpose. For the first time, neither Iraqi equipment nor an Arab scientist were the targets: a company of purely Italian origin had been damaged. The personal attack on Fiorelli's flat meant that those who were behind it meant to give a warning to all the Europeans who were involved in the Iraqi project.

The message left near Fiorelli's flat hinted at a new direction in the campaign against the Iraqi A-bomb. It said, among other things, 'We know about your personal collaboration with the enemies of the Islamic revolution. All those who co-operate with our enemies will be our enemies.' The message went on, demanding the end of SNIA Techint co-operation with the Iraqis to prevent bloodshed. It ended with a personal warning: 'If you don't do this, we will strike out against you and your family without pity.'

Following the attacks in Rome, threatening letters were sent to other European scientists in France, Italy and even Iraq who were involved in the project. The letters to those scientists already working in Al Tuwaitha were sent from Iraq itself. This was not to save money, but mainly to show the European scientists and technicians that those threatening them were also very close to them geographically and that they could carry out their threats if they were not satisfied with the result of the letters.

All the letters were signed by the same group who had claimed responsibility for the bombing in Rome, namely The Committee to Safeguard the Islamic Revolution. The name suggested a pro-Khomeini group in Iraq who felt threatened by the Iraqi project. But security services involved in the investigation were sure that no Iranian group could have carried out such a professional operation. Again Mossad, who had operated a similar mission against Nasser's German scientists at the beginning of the 1960s, was blamed for the job.

Although the blackmail operation was carried out very professionally, it had little effect *per se* on the Iraqi project. Some foreign employees in Iraq had second thoughts concerning the job they were doing. Others ignored it completely. The Iraqi government as well as the French and Italian authorities promised the frightened scientists that they were well protected from the long hand of whoever was behind the attacks.

In the middle of this secret operation, war between Iraq and Iran broke out. Saddam Hussein expected a quick victory over the Iranian forces in a blitz-type campaign. He soon learned that this initiative of his had landed Iraq in a protracted battle and the Iraqi Army proved to be less efficient than its enemies had feared.

9

Final Warning: The Iranian Attack

The war between Khomeini's Iran and Hussein's Iraq began on 21 September 1980. Four days earlier the President of Iraq had announced the cancellation of the 1975 agreement with Iran for mutual use of the 'Shatt al Arab'.

The war had some immediate efforts on the Tammuz project, the first of which took place on 30 September.

Since the start of the war, Iraqi and Iranian fighters had been tactically and strategically bombing each other's targets. The anti-aircraft defence of both states proved to be quite inefficient and Iraqi fighter bombers could quite easily have reached Tehran, while Iranian Phantoms could fly over Baghdad. Though refineries and other oil facilities were bombed from both sides of the border, the Iraqis were sure that the Iranians would never try to bomb the nuclear project in Al Tawita.

In the early hours of the afternoon of 30 September the Iraqis again found out that they were mistaken. Two Iranian F-4 Phantom jets, armoured with rockets and guns, flew low towards Al Tawita, which is just 20km south-east of Baghdad. They shot their rockets and the rest of their ammunition without even a second round of strafing, and disappeared within seconds. The Iraqis did not even have enough time to react. No anti-aircraft missile was launched and the ZSU-23-4 anti-aircraft guns were kept silent.

The damage caused to the 17 Tammuz project was minimal. The reactors themselves were not damaged and only some labs and service facilities were hit. The construction of the water-cooling system of the reactors was damaged by a direct hit from a rocket. Some plumbing installations and piping systems were ruined. A facility for the storing of liquid radioactive wastes was also seriously damaged. The facility for dealing with radioactive wastes was slightly damaged.

Raphael Eitan, the Israeli Chief of Staff, whose intelligence sources in this part of the world were considered to be among the best, evaluated that the project actually survived the first attack on it. Eitan added that the minute the French technicians were back to work the project would be in operation again.

But the attack had delayed the advance of the nuclear project. On the outbreak of war, most of the French experts left Iraq. Immediately after the bombing of the reactor the rest of the foreign technicians, for safety reasons, had to leave Al Tawita and only very few technicians, whose entry to the project area was subject to Iraqi permission, remained.

However, the new situation had some advantages for the Iraqis. They had already operated the small Tammuz II reactor with the first load of 12kg enriched uranium. Since only a small portion of this load had been used, they immediately removed the rest of the fuel from the reactor and kept it in a safe place. Although Iraq had committed itself to French as well as IAEA inspection it now refused any such inspection, claiming that the war with Iran had created a new situation.

Most important of all was the Iranian air attack itself. It indicated to the Iraqis that even their most sensitive project was open to air strike. Now the Iraqis began paying particular attention to the anti-aircraft defence system of the whole project. They knew that if Iranian planes could attack once, they could hit again. In October 1980 Thompson CSF Industries in France signed a $900 million deal with Iraq by which the French company was to set up an electronics industry based at Samara, with initial manufacturing of radio and radar instrumentation for military purposes. By the terms of another deal, for $800 million, France was to supply Iraq with Magique R-500 air-to-air missiles, Exocet missiles and Crotale or Shain surface-to-air missiles. It seems that Iraq was now very anxious about its anti-aircraft defences. In January 1981 another deal was signed with Thompson CSF, by which the French consortium was to supply Iraq with special surface-to-air missiles as well as radar systems which were particularly efficient against American-made electronic systems.

The Iraqis perhaps understood the meaning of the Iranian attack on 30 September 1980. But they could never have guessed what Israel was preparing for them. As the French experts returned to Al Tawita during the winter of 1981, the Israeli Air Force was already preparing its pre-emptive strike against the Iraqi Tammuz project.

10

The Trio Decide

Despite its secret and unique nature, the decision to destroy the Iraqi nuclear reactor was taken in the full cabinet form some time in October 1980. Decisions of this kind in Israel had been made in the past either by one person – Ben Gurion in 1956 – or the informal Labour inner circle (Golda's Kitchen Cabinet) or small ministerial committees for security (which would include the prime minister, the defence, foreign and treasury ministers and sometimes the chief of staff and chief of IDF intelligence). It had been preceded by serious debates, discussions and efforts to turn every stone to prevent French–Iraqi nuclear collaboration. The Labour government of Rabin (1974–77) and his Defence Minister Shimon Peres had already agonized on the best political and diplomatic strategy to follow and, if this was fruitless, what military strategy Israel should adopt to prevent the creation of a military nuclear reactor in Iraq. No timing was set for D-Day, but the instruments of war – Air Force, operations section in GHQ and Intelligence – started planning several contingencies and training for the operation.

It was clear from the first discussions of the General Staff Senior Officers Forum,[1] which began some time in late summer or early autumn of 1980, that the opinions of the 10–12 officers present were almost equally divided.

The main argument of those who opposed the attack was that even if it succeeded it would not destroy the 12kg of weapon-grade enriched uranium the French were known to have already supplied to the Iraqis, nor the smaller amount of enriched uranium the Iraqis might have acquired from elsewhere. It was also known that later on the French were to

supply the Iraqis with yet another 12kg of weapon-grade uranium, which had been deposited somewhere in a heavily-pro-
tected concrete pyramid (covered over by 24 feet of concrete)
and that there was no way either to destroy or get control over
this uranium. The fear of those objecting to the raid was, therefore, that even if it was successful, the Iraqis would still be able
to go ahead and produce a nuclear bomb – and might in fact
even have an increased incentive to do so.

Those who supported the raid replied that the amount of
weapon-grade uranium in Iraqi hands was not enough to produce even one bomb. They argued that if the Iraqis were
allowed to activate the reactor they would be able to acquire
much larger quantities of weapon-grade uranium (perhaps up
to 36kg per year), which would be used to operate the reactor
and which would finally produce a considerable amount of plutonium – enough to produce two or three bombs a year. If the
reactor was destroyed *before* it was activated and *before* the
additional 12kg were supplied by the French, then the Iraqis
would not be able to produce a nuclear bomb (or at most one,
if the calculations were wrong) until they put into operation the
plutonium route to the bomb. Moreover, they argued, following such an attack, the French and Italians might be reluctant to
rebuild the Iraqi reactor and, if they did, would impose much
stricter controls on the supply and use of the weapon-grade
uranium and/or the retrieval of the plutonium produced by the
reactor.

Those in favour of the attack on the reactor, including
among them Chief of Staff Raphael Eitan, finally won the
debate by a small margin and it was decided to go ahead with
the planning of the operation. Around this time two Israeli
engineers visited the US and consulted American nuclear
experts on what would happen to a nuclear reactor if attacked
by 1,000kg bombs.

The debate over timing had two interrelated aspects – when
would the Iraqi reactor become 'hot' and when should the military option be employed? When the government's October
decision became known to leading members of the Labour
Party, Peres and Gur, this external debate over timing immediately became entangled in electoral politics.

Earlier the Labour government and its leaders had sought

more time for diplomacy, although in 1977 when they had lost the election the military purposes of Osirak had not as yet been determined. Peres in particular, as a prime mover of Israel's nuclear reactor in Dimona between 1958 and 1965, must have felt even in May 1981 that the Iraqi reactor was not, as yet, critical and that the rise of President Mitterrand, a Socialist and personal friend, could prove diplomatically advantageous to Israel *vis-à-vis* French–Iraqi activities.

Thus in May 1981, when Peres was still leading in the pre-election polls, he wrote and sent the following letter to Begin at the traditional Sunday Israeli cabinet meeting:

May 10

PERSONAL – TOP SECRET

Mr Prime Minister

At the end of December 1980 you called me into your office in Jerusalem and told me about a certain extremely serious matter.[2] You did not solicit to my response and I myself (despite my instinctive feeling) did not respond in the circumstances that then existed.

I feel this morning that it is my supreme civic duty to advise you, after serious consideration and in weighing the national interest, to desist from this thing.

I speak as a man of experience. The deadines[3] reported by us (and I well understand our people's anxiety) are not the realistic deadlines.[4] Material can be changed for (other) material.[5] And what is intended to prevent can become a catalyst.[6]

On the other hand Israel would be like a tree in the desert – and we also have that to be concerned about.[7]

I add my voice – and it is not mine alone[8] – to the voices of those who tell you not to do it,[9] and certainly not at the present time in the present circumstances.

Respectfully,
Shimon Peres

The surprised and furious Begin, now finding that the October decision was no longer a closely kept secret, showed the letter to M.K. Moshe Arens, Chairman of the Foreign and Security Committee. The October decision was no longer the property of a select few – in addition to Peres, former Defence Minister Weizman, a former Chief of Staff, Mordechai (Mota) Gur, two Israeli journalists and one businessman close to Weizman were also acquainted with the projected raid.

The revelation of 10 May 1981 that the decision to destroy the reactor had taken place in October 1980 imposed on Begin and his inner circle the necessity to choose another date from that set previously. Begin was aware that the US intelligence community now knew of Israel's intentions and apprehensions. He also knew that if he lost the election, the Opposition would be less than keen to pursue the plan immediately.

To ensure no further leakage, and to ensure a positive vote his way, Begin set up a small group that would be heremetically safe to make sure that security would be preserved. This was the so-called Committee of the Three, composed of Begin himself, Eitan and Shamir. Others were consulted about the new date, such as Yadin and Deputy Defence Minister Zipori, yet the 'pushers', the most avid advocates of the raid that had finally been moved to 7 June 1981, were Begin, 'superhawk' Sharon and Eitan. Most of the debate was actually between 'Begin and Begin'. For him the threat of the Nazi-like Saddam Hussein was clear. The trauma of the Holocaust and Begin's several gulags had been resurrected as he imagined the death of half a million Jews from an Iraqi bomb which Begin was in no doubt Hussein would use when it was ready. For Begin the Jewish historical tragedy and the trauma – personal and collective – of the Holocaust were clearly the triggers that made him decide to annihilate the Iraqi reactor on 7 June 1981.

NOTES

1. The General Staff Senior Officers Forum is the highest and most important decision-making group of the Israeli Defence Forces, concerned with policy, long-range military build-up and any important large-scale military operational decisions. It comprises all the heads of the military branches and active-duty officers from the rank of major-general upwards (including all the heads of the air force, navy, armoured corps, military intelligence, area or district commanders, quartermaster general, the head of the operation section, the chief of staff himself and, depending on the subject matter discussed, the head of

Mossad, the Minister of Defence and his deputy or other key personalities – in general only the minimum number of people will be present). The discussions are held on an open and democratic basis rather than on rank or seniority. The Chief of Staff is the *primus inter pares* and probably has, *de facto*, the power of veto. In other words, it is safe to assume that action or decisions will not be taken against his explicit and formidable authority.

2. Peres tends to use euphemisms when discussing very sensitive matters. This secret letter is full of such euphemisms. The following are their explanations: Israel's intention to move up another step in its efforts to stop the Iraqi nuclear project, i.e. to bomb it.

3. The time in which the reactor will become 'hot', according to which Begin's cabinet decided to make the raid.

4. The operation of the reactor is not (according to Peres' sources) immediate. There is still time for diplomatic and other types of activities against the Iraqi project.

5. Ninety-three per cent enriched uranium. This military-grade uranium is the nuclear fuel for the Osiris-type reactor. It might also refer to parts of the reactor which would be damaged in the raid but would be replaced by France. Peres hints here that the solution is a political and not a military one.

6. The aim of the Israeli raid is to prevent Iraq and other Arab states from becoming nuclear states. This operation, however, might cause them to intensify their efforts because it would show how Israel is attempting nuclear monopoly in the Middle East.

7. An allusion to Israel's own nuclear efforts. Peres is worried that the raid might focus world attention on Israel's nuclear option, which is against its interest.

8. Peres leaked the information to some other senior members in his party. Among them were Rabin and Gur (both ex-chiefs of staff of the IDF) and Abba Eban (ex-Foreign Affairs Minister). All were against the raid.

9. Some cabinet members were against the raid – and not only its timing – as were some others, mainly in the army. Peres shows here that it was not only a matter of the opposition *vis-à-vis* Begin's coalition, but a much broader problem.

PART THREE

*THE PREPARATIONS FOR OPERATION
BABYLON*

11

Operation Babylon: Options

The codename was 'Ammunition Hill'. It was to be a 'two-minute Entebbe-style raid' – a surgical attack against the Iraqi Tammuz 17 (originally called Osirak) 70 megawatt nuclear reactor, located in the nuclear research centre at Al Tawita, 20km south-east of Baghdad.

All military experts know that behind every complex military operation – even of brief duration and perfect execution – lie many months of intense preparation. Each complex operation requires precise planning and staff work, attention to minute and trivial detail. There is the continuous need to revise and update the procedures of each plan, to find the commanders and soldiers most suitable for its implementation, and the optimal equipment to carry out the operation; special equipment often has to be designed and prepared for the specific task, careful maintenance work carried out; and last but not least, the success of each military operation requires hard work and endless training. Only after all the necessary preparations have been meticulously carried out can the operation have a realistic chance of success.

Only rarely, if and when a military operation dismally fails (such as the US rescue operation in Iran, 1980), or years later when historians have access to classified documents, can the non-expert glimpse the details of such preparations.

The two-minute raid on Tammuz (Osirak) was the culmination of a long and hard planning-and-preparation process that reflects the character and history of the Israeli Air Force (IAF). The IAF, which in the early 1980s was both qualitatively and quantitatively the third largest air force in the world and the most experienced in modern air tactics and warfare, has a long tradition of thorough preparation for its apparently facile, brilliant and lightning quick operations. There was the destruction of the Arab Air Force on the ground in the first three hours of the Six Day War;[1] the IAF operation as a flying artillery during the war of attrition; the heist of a Soviet-made radar station from Egypt in a daring raid;[2] the shooting of five of the most experienced Soviet fighter pilots at the end of the war of attrition over Egypt; the brilliant performance following the Egyptian and Syrian surprise attack across the Suez Canal and the Golan Heights – when the IAF, all alone for the first two days, tried to block the onslaught of the two attacking armies, the kill ratio in dogfights achieved during the Yom Kippur War being 55-to-1 in its favour;[3] and, last but not least, the central contribution of the IAF to the success of the Israeli rescue operation at Entebbe.

After the Israeli military Intelligence and Mossad[4] received alarming information during the spring and summer of 1980 concerning the rapid progress made by the Iraqis with the aid of the French and Italians in the work on their nuclear 'research' programme – and it became clear that Iraq might be able to design and produce first a crude nuclear device and later nuclear weapons ahead of the expected schedule (it had earlier been estimated that the Iraqis would not be able to produce nuclear weapons before 1985, a forecast the CIA refused to change contrary to Israeli intelligence experts' opinion in the autumn of 1980) – the Israeli government and the General Staff knew that some pre-emptive action to destroy Iraqi nuclear capability would have to be taken before it was too late.

Israel could choose among four possibilities to achieve this goal:

(1) To intensify the diplomatic campaign against the Western states supplying Iraq with the nuclear know-how and material or, alternatively, solicit their support in halting Iraq's progress on its nuclear project. And/or:
(2) To carry out an intensified clandestine type of operation against Iraq and those supporting it.
(3) To undertake an all-out combined commando-type operation against the Iraqi nuclear facilities in Al Tawita.

(4) To launch a surgical attack from the air.

It appeared as though an intensified diplomatic campaign against France, Italy, Brazil, Portugal, Nigeria or Libya – all of which had contributed in one form or another to the Iraqi nuclear effort – would not be very successful. So far the Israeli diplomatic campaign, which had started as early as 1977, had not yielded any results. Iraq had the money, the oil and the business which those countries needed. When the French tried to convince the Iraqis to purchase another type of nuclear fuel – Caramel[5] – the Iraqis refused point-blank even to listen, and the French, who feared risking not only their huge arms sales to Iraq (France supplied a quarter of all Iraqi weapons) but also the nuclear deal and a secure source of oil supplies, quickly yielded under Iraqi counter-pressure. In fact both Italy and France kept on passing the buck to each other. The Italians claimed that their chemical plant (i.e. the separation plant for plutonium) was useless without the French Tammuz 17 nuclear reactor, that therefore the French were to blame and that it was the French who must break their deal with Iraq. Meanwhile the French were claiming that without the Italian 'chemical' separation plant no nuclear weapons could be produced. This impasse did not change under the half-hearted diplomatic pressure on the US government which Israel had to mobilize. A continued and even intensified diplomatic campaign had little prospect of success against French and Italian hypocrisy and greed. At best an intensified diplomatic campaign would make the governments of both countries feel a little more guilty and force them to continue their deals with the Iraqis under even stricter conditions of secrecy. Moreover, diplomatic campaigns can take a considerable time to mature until they have the desired effect: in the meantime the Iraqis might be able to reach the point of no return some time in the summer of 1981 and would quite possibly *activate the nuclear reactor and the Italian separation plant*.

To all intents and purposes, therefore, the time factor set a limit on the diplomatic option.

Concerning clandestine activities, there is no certain proof of the use of these methods. However, the international press reported activities of this type such as the successful explosion of the core of the Iraqi–French-built reactor shortly before it was to be removed from a warehouse in Seyne-sur-Mer to be shipped to Iraq; the murder a year later of the Egyptian-born nuclear physicist, head of Iraq's nuclear programme, in his hotel room in Paris; the bombing of the Rome offices of SNIA-Techint, the Italian nuclear company that was supplying the Iraqis with the separation plant; and finally a reported attempt to assassinate a French scientist working on the Osirak project in Paris.

All this served the purpose of deterring individual experts in Italy and France from joining such projects: they were meant to signal to the governments involved that those governments had better do something about it. Finally, such activities – in particular the sabotage of the core of the Iraqi nuclear reactor – were intended to delay Iraqi progress in its nuclear project as much as possible.

In the final analysis, however, all the dirty tricks had only a limited, delaying impact at the tactical level and only a marginal effect on the long-range nuclear ambitions of the Iraqi government.

The possibility of destroying or sabotaging the Iraqi nuclear reactor from within was allegedly discussed too – and probably rejected as a highly risky and dangerous undertaking. To have done this effectively would have required a large amount of explosives. Such a quantity could not possibly have been smuggled into this closely guarded area. Each of the foreign (as well as local) technicians was carefully searched and examined at least twice upon entering the facility. Special devices (such as the one installed in many airports today that can X-ray attaché cases and sniff out even the smallest trace of high explosives) were installed in the first and second checkpoints. Once within the working area foreign workers were closely watched by Iraqi security men dressed in camouflage uniform and green berets, carrying Soviet AK-47 assault rifles with folded metal butts. Other guards in civilian clothes, many of whom spoke Italian and French, were also on the premises. Finally, the whole area was under continual surveillance by close-circuit TV cameras and probably other devices too.

It was also suspected that some of the foreign workers were acting as agents for the Iraqis and earning an extra salary by keeping a close eye on their colleagues. The whole nuclear area itself was surrounded by a concrete wall as well as by a lower electrical fence, which could immediately alert the guards located in special control rooms when it was breached. And, finally, the perimeter was under continuous surveillance by armed patrols in British landrovers and American sedans.

Even if, despite all these precautionary measures, one of the technicians or engineers who were working as double agents for Israel (and there must have been several – and each would not have known who the others were) could have smuggled a small quantity of high explosives into the working area, it surely would have been much too small to be effective, and once in the working area it would have been extremely difficult to prepare the charge under the close watch of the many known and unknown guards. It goes without saying that anyone caught in any such attempt would have been summarily tortured and executed. To collect and report information involves risks enough, but to attempt to sabotage the closely guarded facility from within was quite another matter. Not even the most daring and dedicated agent – let alone mercenary – would have considered such a suicidal mission, which in any event could have caused only minor damage.

Finally, the Israelis probably considered that by avoiding a clandestine operation and opting instead for a fully-fledged attack, they would be able to deter foreign governments from continued participation in this project. The possibility of a *direct* clandestine operation of sabotage was therefore rejected from the outset.

NOTES

1. Altogether some 451 Arab warplanes were destroyed (most of them on the ground) during the Six Day War. Israel lost some 50 warplanes, mostly to anti-aircraft fire.
2. This raid against Station P-12, which followed the IAF in its operation over Egypt, was carried out on the night of 26 December 1969. Israeli soldiers had been training for a few days on older models of similar Soviet radars. The radar was cut in half and hoisted across the Gulf of Suez to the Sinai. The story of the raid was first disclosed by the *Daily Express* on 3 January 1970 under the headline 'Israel Stole Seven Tons of Secrets'.
3. The IAF success during the Yom Kippur War can be measured by the fact that despite the success of the Egyptian–Syrian surprise attack no Arab planes successfully penetrated or attacked Israel's territory during the war while Israel

continually attacked targets in Egypt and Syria. In the course of the war, the IAF destroyed 514 Arab warplanes, most of them in air battles (334); the rest were lost to ground fire (158) and on the ground (22). Israel lost some 102 warplanes, almost all of them to anti-aircraft missiles and guns.

4. Israeli military intelligence is the largest intelligence organization in Israel, in terms of budget, manpower, and material resources. It is responsible for national security. It collects, sifts and analyses all intelligence concerned primarily with the Arab states on the borders of Israel and in direct military conflict with Israel. The Mossad is the Israeli equivalent of the CIA. It is primarily concerned with longer-range covert intelligence operations beyond the immediate states bordering on Israel.

5. The Caramel-type fuel is not suitable for the production of nuclear weapons – although in the later stage of its use part of it is transformed into plutonium, which could be used to produce atomic weapons.

12

Operation Babylon: A Second Entebbe?

Another possible course of action open to Israeli planners was a direct long-range combined operation assault on the reactor carried out from an Israeli base by elite Israeli troops, possibly disguised as Iraqi soldiers, many of whom could speak fluent Arabic in an Iraqi dialect. Such a programme must have appealed to Raphael Eitan, the Israeli Chief of Staff who was particularly interested in this type of operation, and to many of Israel's top commando officers – although it had less appeal to officers whose background was more conventional and technical men from the armed corps or from the IAF.

As we know now, it was not the final strategy chosen and for a good many reasons.

A long-range commando raid of some 550 miles in each direction is not easy even under the most ideal conditions. A similar raid across one of the most arid and inhospitable deserts in the world, in difficult terrain which offers few, if any, places to hide and against an enemy who is at war (and therefore on the alert) is a very risky enterprise, raising extremely difficult logistical and technical questions.

Its planning can generally be divided into three stages: the approach to the objective; the attack on the installation itself; and the withdrawal. Each of these stages raises a host of different problems requiring different solutions, different participants and a plethora of special means. The planning of each stage involves solutions to a myriad of intricate problems and it is also necessary to be prepared for a variety of unexpected developments and complications. Dangerous surprises need not arise out of cataclysmic events or counter-attacks but from small and seemingly unimportant items or events, such as the lack of sand filters on the CH-53 Sea Stallion helicopters that carried the US rescue team to Iran and which led to the decision to abort the mission. No doubt the tragic end of the US raid on Iran was foremost in the minds of *all* of the Israeli planners of the long-range commando raid against the Iraqi reactor. Any mistake on the approach to the target, the attack on the target itself or the withdrawal could result in the death or capture of hundreds of soldiers and expensive equipment. The ever-present probability of the unexpected, the small or large mistake that could lead to a disaster, is known only too well to anyone who has participated in the planning and, even more, the execution of such raids.

The success of the raid on Entebbe, though it had created a precedent for such an operation, paradoxically made a repeat performance far more difficult.

In the first place, Entebbe was the first long-range rescue operation of its kind ever attempted. As such it was deemed impossible to undertake and therefore was totally unexpected – and surprise in this case *was* the essence of success. But as is well-known in military affairs, and life in general, one cannot always play the same trick twice and hope to succeed.

The American raid on Iran came not only second but also against a very different background. Unlike those in Entebbe, which was situated outside Kampala in an isolated area with little defence, the American hostages in Tehran were in the heart of a major metropolis under heavy guard. Moreover, the American plan lacked the elegance of the Israeli Entebbe raid. It involved personnel from too many branches of the US armed forces, too many points of refuelling and other preparations. It involved landing near a major highway, and the means of arrival were different from the means of departure. The whole operation would also have necessitated heavy fighting.

The US rescue operation was an act of desperation rather than of rational military planning. It had no chance of success whatsoever.

The Israeli soldiers and officers who would participate in the raid and its planning were among the most experienced in the world, and with literally hundreds of such operations behind them knew only too well the high risks involved.

Any large-scale operation of this kind would have involved *at least* 200 (but probably more) soldiers and pilots who would have to be carried over long distances. The range of even the largest Israeli helicopter would not have sufficed to cover that distance both ways. Therefore, either the helicopters carrying the troops would have required refuelling somewhere on the way to the target or before the attack on the target (probably at night), a complicated operation in which the helicopters and their crews would be highly vulnerable to any counter-attack if detected. Moreover, the refuelling process would require the presence of other cargo airlift airplanes to carry the necessary fuel and these would have to land undetected somewhere in the enemy's territory. Again, given their size and the fact that Iraq was at war with Iran and at least on partial alert, this would not be easy to achieve.

While the undetected approach of such huge aircraft is very difficult if not impossible, the Israelis, given their knack for stratagems and deception, would certainly have tried to protect the approach of their aircraft by some ruse or another: either, for example, by masquerading as commercial aircraft on international air-traffic approaches or by pretending to be Iraqi aircraft or the aircraft of some other friendly Arab or foreign state. Other deception tactics were surely considered as well.

Furthermore, large and vulnerable cargo aircraft would need the cover of fighter aircraft at least on the way back (if not on the way in) after the attack on the target had taken place and the enemy was in hot pursuit of the attackers. Such large aircraft would require adequate landing strips, ground-to-air co-ordination, maintenance specialists and the like.

Large cargo aircraft would be required not only for refuelling the helicopters but also possibly to carry some of the smaller helicopters, which would themselves be needed to transport the commandos straight into the target area. It is reasonable to assume that the fastest and safest way to overcome the Iraqi defences *around* the reactor would have been by using smaller helicopters flying at tree-top level to leapfrog right into the heart of the nuclear research centre.

The major flaw of such a plan lies of course in the extreme vulnerability of helicopters to any ground-to-air fire. Therefore, while the helicopters could, if total surprise were to be achieved, have successfully penetrated the defence perimeter around the reactor, safely landed the commandos on the target and safely cleared the area, it is highly unlikely that they could have also been used to lift out the withdrawing attacking force.

Another approach to the reactor could have been to have Israeli commandos driving a convoy of trucks, jeeps and troop carriers carrying the insignia of the Iraqi Army. Some of these convoy trucks could have been flown in by the Israeli Air Force (IAF) cargo airplanes (such as the Hercules C-130), while others could have been purchased or obtained locally by special agents arriving (or living) in the Baghdad area weeks before. The attacking commandos could have been dropped by parachute over the target. Parachute operations, as is well known, are extremely delicate and tricky. Paratroops are highly vulnerable while in the air (as are the aircraft carrying them), they and their equipment disperse on the ground and require considerable time to regroup. In other words, the safe and effective approach of commando troops across the desert to a well-protected target seemed to impose almost insurmountable problems.

The second phase of such an operation would naturally be the attack on the target itself and its destruction. The attacking forces would have had at their disposal detailed plans and blueprints of the Osirak nuclear reactor, perhaps even the active guidance of one or more of the experts who worked at the facility, the best possible, up-to-the-minute information on the defensive installations around and within the reactor, the number of guards, patrols, their weapons, their means of communication with their headquarters and the like. The attacking troops themselves would probably have held many mock and practice rehearsal attacks on a detailed model of the reactor. The operation would not have taken place unless those responsible for the rehearsal training judged that the troops were ready and would have a reasonable chance to succeed in their mission and return safely to Israel.

But, as already emphasized, such operations always involved much that is unknown and unexpected. In any event, an assault on such a well-protected target could only have been achieved at high cost to both the defenders and the attackers as well as to any of the foreign experts working in the reactor during the attack. The large number of casualties to be expected clearly reduced its possible appeal to the political and military leaders of Israel, who were afraid for the lives of the attacking commandos themselves (Israeli hypersensitivity to casualties is well known) and afraid that, if a large number of Iraqi scientists and other civilians or, even worse, foreign experts were killed, Israel would be charged by the world's mass media and kind souls with using unnecessary force and killing innocent civilian bystanders. (It must of course be remembered that, from Israel's point of view, anyone participating in the production of weapons of mass destruction such as atomic bombs, with a brutal enemy in a state of war with Israel, cannot be considered as an innocent civilian. From this point of view, the more Iraqi nuclear experts who could be killed the better. It would mean that Iraq's capacity to produce nuclear weapons could be reduced considerably – and that its nuclear weapons project would be delayed for an indefinite period of time.)

Such considerations, in fact, required that the attack should be carried out on a normal working day, when as many as possible of Iraq's nuclear experts would be working at the nuclear research centre. The difficulty with this approach was that normally, while the Iraqi experts were present at the reactor, all the other foreign experts would also be there. The difficulty in distinguishing between the Iraqi, French and Italian experts would have caused many casualties among the Europeans. And this Israel wanted to avoid as much as possible. Indeed, as was shown later by the choice of the air attack on the reactor, the Israelis were extremely careful not to cause any casualties among foreign experts.[1]

Finally, came the last but not least important stage, withdrawal. The commandos, after having hopefully destroyed the nuclear reactor, would have had to leave the reactor area as quickly as possible. A lot would of course have depended on the speed with which they could get control of the reactor and make their preparations to blow it up. (They might even have received instructions to take away with them most of the weapon-grade enriched uranium to be found in or near the reactor. For this of course a team of Israeli nuclear scientists who were also trained as commando officers would have been included in the raiding party. It was, however, known to Israeli intelligence that at that time the weapon-grade uranium was not stored at the nuclear research area but in another even more heavily guarded area: more on this will be said.)

The speed of the operation would be critical. From the moment the assault was started it could be assumed that the Iraqi general staff headquarters in Baghdad, the internal security forces and its air forces would be alerted and their counter-moves would start to take place. The faster the goals of the raid could be accomplished – still in total darkness – the quicker and safer the withdrawal. The commandos would probably have taken either the helicopters, which would fly in again, or alternatively have left the area in the trucks waiting outside. By either method they would have had to reach the longer-range aircraft that would carry them back home.

The aircraft themselves (if they were to wait on the ground throughout the raid) would risk being detected. If so, it would be very easy for the Iraqis to block their way out. If not, they could quickly take off and, although probably flying at a height of only 100 feet (highly dangerous by itself), they might be discovered and intercepted by Iraqi fighter-interceptors either over Iraq or as far away as Jordan. To protect and cover the slow and heavy cargo aircraft at night over Iraqi skies would be next to impossible.

Such a three-stage plan was much too complicated and risky. And if it was explored for a while by the Israeli Army and the Mossad, the Israeli planners decided that a commando raid on the ground would not work – the probability of failure was too high. They were looking for a much simpler, safer and quicker operation with a minimum number of points of friction and things that could go wrong. They were, so to speak, looking for the shortest distance between two points and not a multi-stage and complex operation.

They finally decided to turn the planning of the raid over to the Israeli Air Force, provided that the IAF could guarantee the destruction of the reactor by a surgical strike from the air. The total destruction of the nuclear reactor would in that case be achieved at the lowest risk to human lives and the smallest damage to Israel in terms of world public opinion.

A senior IAF officer once told a journalist interviewing him about the success of the IAF that the guiding principle behind the operations of the air force could be summarized in the simple word KISS – *Keep it Simple, Stupid.* This cardinal principle the Pentagon people chose to ignore when planning the US rescue operation in Iran.

A special task force of the best minds in the operation branch of the IAF was now assigned to find the most 'simple' but effective plan to destroy the Iraqi nuclear reactor.

NOTE

1. The date chosen was a Sunday, so it was assumed that the European experts would not be working on that day. This turned out to be the only known blunder to be made by Israeli Intelligence since foreign experts took Friday, the Muslim Sabbath, as a rest day but worked on Sundays. The hour for the attack itself was chosen as the best hour to approach the target from the *west* when the sun would be setting in the west and would shine directly into the eyes of the anti-aircraft defences of the Iraqis. It was not chosen because the workers had already finished their work and gone home, because it was wrongly assumed that on that day they did not work at all. As it happened, at the hour of the attack – 18.30 Iraqi time – most workers had already gone home and only one French expert was inadvertently killed. Had the attack taken place at an earlier time or in the winter when the sun sets earlier, it is possible that many foreign and Iraqi experts would have been killed.

13

Operation Babylon: Reconnaissance

The man chosen to lead the co-ordination between the Israeli Air Force (IAF), Mossad, Military Intelligence, General Staff headquarters and the planning of the raid was Colonel Aviem Sella, the head of the IAF Planning Branch in the early 1980s. Sella, who would later become known as the handler of Jonathan Pollard, the US intelligence officer caught delivering sensitive nformation to the Israelis, was known to be a brilliant officer and an excellent pilot of considerable experience. In addition to fighting the Arabs in the 1967 Six Day War, the War of Attrition over the Suez Canal (October 1968–August 1970), and the Yom Kippur War of 1973, Sella was one of the few pilots in the world with combat experience of fighting Soviet pilots. In July 1970, at the height of the War of Attrition, he had participated in a dog fight with MIG-21s flown by Soviet pilots, who had come to assist their Egyptian clients. At the end of this fight, five Soviets had been shot down with no Israeli casualties. In those wars he gained experience in flying the French Mirage III, the small but highly versatile US-made bomber, the Skyhawk A-4 (the work-horse of the Israeli 'flying artillery'), and finally the F-4 Phantom fighter bomber, the heaviest warplane of the Israeli Air Force until the arrival of the F-15.

Although he had been serving as a staff officer responsible for the operation at IAF HQ for almost two years from the day of decision, Sella kept himself in shape as a pilot in close touch with the real action by flying and training at least once a week. This is a tradition that even the highest-ranking Israeli Air Force officers observe.

Sella, like most IAF officers was relatively young – only 38 years old. For many years, he had to remain anonymous and the only visiting card he left behind was at the end of the successful raid on the Iraqi nuclear reactor.

One thing is clear: Sella was one of the most brilliant planning minds of the Israeli Air Force, a man who believed in the central role of air power in modern warfare and who maintained that, limitations notwithstanding, air power was the most cost-effective form of military power if properly used and understood. In the planning and execution of Operation Babylon he saw a golden opportunity to demonstrate this; his beliefs coincided with the powerful bureaucratic political interest in the IAF, not only to justify continued investment in it (well over 50 per cent of the military budget) but perhaps also to hint that in fact this budget had to be increased even further.

As soon as it was agreed to opt for an air attack, the IAF planning team went into high gear. All the data necessary for the attack had to be collected and put together, from Military Intelligence, Mossad, air force intelligence – and of course all those agencies were trying to do the best they could to obtain additional information.

Israeli intelligence had accumulated a dossier on Iraq's nuclear capabilities and intentions since 1975, which has been continuously updated. Although this dossier had grown considerably to the proportions of a couple of thick volumes, even more up-to-date information was required. The Mossad in particular, and Military Intelligence, doubled their efforts to obtain information from agents in the field and probably increased their efforts to recruit foreign nuclear experts working in Iraq. Following the Iranian raid on the Iraqi nuclear reactor on 30 September 1980, the French and Italian experts at first returned to their own countries (but went back in February 1981 to work at the Iraqi nuclear reactor where full-scale work began some time in April 1981). This development probably gave Mossad an opportunity to recruit some of the top experts to its service.[1]

Up-to-date information was needed on a large number of questions: the progress of work at the nuclear site; the whereabouts or storage place of the French weapon-grade enriched uranium in Iraq; the defences – air and other types – around the nuclear reactor which had been boosted following the Iranian attack of 30 September 1980; the radar defences of Iraq, Saudi Arabia and Jordan; detailed weather and climatic conditions over the target; the exact amounts of explosives necessary to assure the destruction of the reactor; and many other questions.

Some time during October 1980, again following the Iranian attack on the reactor, the Israeli Air Force probably obtained permission[2] to send a high-altitude reconnaissance[3] flight over the reactor to take air photographs and make an infra-red photographic survey of the reactor's area.[4]

The Israelis were certainly curious as to the amount of damage caused to the Iraqi reactor, how much such damage could delay the Iraqi nuclear programme and the extent of reinforcements of the Iraqi anti-aircraft defences around the reactor following the Iranian air raid.

Some time during the autumn of 1980 representatives of the Israeli intelligence community met with their US colleagues – CIA and DIA (Defense Intelligence Agency) – in Washington DC to exchange views on the progress of the Iraqi nuclear programme. The Americans did not share the immediate concern of their Israeli colleagues, although they did express worries over the danger of Iraq obtaining nuclear weapons in the longer run. They told their worried Israeli visitors that according to their estimates the Iraqis could not obtain any nuclear weapons or a nuclear device before 1985 or 1986. The Israelis, probably projecting their own nuclear experience, were afraid the Iraqis would obtain such weapons much earlier. It is highly possible that on that occasion the Israelis had obtained US satellite reconnaissance photographs of the reactor's area.

It was also rumoured that around this time (but possibly also much earlier) that the Israelis had obtained aerial photographs from Savak (Iranian Intelligence). The Israelis had had close connections with Savak since the mid-1950s, having trained Iranian intelligence officers and sold weapons to the Iranians. Although, after the Iranian Muslim revolution and the rise of the Ayatollah Khomeini to power, all official relations with Iran were terminated and the Israeli Embassy in Iran was closed (the Israeli Embassy building having been handed over to the PLO), it was rumoured that the two governments continued to maintain some kind of under-the-table contact and that the Israelis were selling the Iranians ammunition and spare parts for their American-made weapons. Moreover, both Israel and Iran (as was recognized by the Shah) had a strong common interest in undermining Iraqi nuclear ambitions, which were probably (Saddam Hussein's statements to the contrary notwithstanding) directed as much against Iran as against Israel.

After all, Iran was a much older enemy than Israel, against which Iraq had long-standing territorial claims. Moreover, while Iran could not retaliate in kind and therefore could not expect to defeat the Iraqis, the Iraqis must have assumed that Israel was at least as advanced as they were in the development of nuclear weapons and therefore could retaliate in kind. The Iraqi surprise attack on Iran in September 1980 created an even stronger incentive for collaboration between the two states. It may therefore be assumed that the Iranians gave the Israelis whatever information they had on the Iraqi nuclear facilities near Baghdad, in the best Middle Eastern tradition that 'the enemy of my enemy is my friend'. The Israelis – unlike the Americans, whose intelligence estimates projected completion of the Osirak project by 1985 – felt pressured for time, so as the information kept coming in they started to train simultaneously with the planning effort, long before the plans for the raid were finished.

Planning raised a few serious problems, the first of which arose out of the long distance to Baghdad from the IAF bases. The *air* distance from the major Israeli air bases Etzion and Eitam in the Sinai (Etzion is near Eilat and Eitam is further north) is over 600 nautical miles (or over 1,000 kilometres) from Baghdad, or, if compared to Britain's bombing missions on Fortress Europe during World War II, it is similar to the distance from London to Berlin, Dresden, Prague, Vienna, Milan or Marseilles – in other words, at the extreme range of the heavy four-engined bombers of World War II.

This distance would mean that the Israeli Air Force would have to undertake *the longest bombing raid in its history*.[5]

NOTES

1. It is of course well known that from an intelligence point of view it is easier to penetrate underdeveloped and less industrialized countries, which depend heavily on foreign experts whose loyalties they cannot fully check or control and whose private goals are of course to make as much money as possible in the shortest possible time.

2. Any long-range reconnaissance flight over an enemy's territory by the Israeli Air Force has to be authorized by the prime minister or defence minister himself (Begin at this stage performed both roles).

3. Israel acquired during the 1970s 12 high-altitude flying RF-4E Phantom reconnaissance planes originally equipped with special photographic and other highly sensitive sensors. It can be assumed that the Israelis further improved and modernized those aircraft. In addition, for shorter-range reconnaissance work the IAF makes heavy use of a variety of remotely piloted vehicles (RPVs) and Drones. As Israel was producing its own highly sophisticated attack and fighter aircraft (the Kfir C-2) it would not be surprising if they had also developed a lighter and higher-flying reconnaissance version of this aircraft.

4. While regular photographs could show any exterior advances in the project, infra-red photographs highly sensitive to any heat sources could 'penetrate' the buildings and see if any machines or heat-producing chemical processes were in operation.

5. Until the raid on the Iraqi nuclear reactor the longest *bombing* raid of the Israeli Air Force was during the Six Day War in 1967 against Egyptian air bases in upper Egypt at Ras Banas (on the Red Sea near the Sudanese border) and Luxor on the upper part of the Nile. The longest range aircraft in Israel's arsenal at that time were the French Votour fighter bombers, whose range was limited. Israeli pilots had at times to fly on *one engine* in order to save fuel and reach upper Egypt. The Israeli Air Force had not developed air refuelling techniques by 1967.

14

Operation Babylon: The Eagle and the Fighting Falcon

When the planners of the attack on the nuclear reactor in Iraq examined the capabilities they could obtain and rely on from the Israeli Air Force, they could be quite satisfied.

Israeli's most important fighting arm had gone through a few dramatic changes reflecting the lessons of the Yom Kippur War.

In 1973, the IAF was not fully ready for the type of attack launched by the Syrian and Egyptian armies. In 1967, the Israeli planes launched a surprise attack against the Arab airfields, thus destroying most of the Arab fighters and bombers (about 350 of them) on the ground in the first hours of the war. By 1973, however, political constraints prevented it from resorting to a similar pre-emptive strike.

The result for the air force was quite catastrophic. In the first days of the war, more than fifty planes were shot down by the Egyptian and Syrian anti-aircraft defence, mainly S-A 6 SAM missiles and ZSU-23-4 mobile anti-aircraft guns.

Political limitations were of course one of the main reasons why the Israeli pilots had to fight under much more difficult conditions. But when the war came to an end, Israeli analysts had to admit that some basic mistakes made in preparing the air force for the next war had been a factor in the initial high rate of attrition. Immediately following the war, they sat down to plan the next one, if and when it was to come.

By the 1980s the Israelis had invested a great deal of work and effort to overcome their main weaknesses.

The main, and the most important change, was the quantitative one. In 1973, on the eve of the October war, the Israelis had about 340 fighters and fighter bombers, primarily F-4s (Phantoms), A-4s (Skyhawks), Mirage III-Cs and their younger brother, the Israeli-made Nesher. They even had to put back into service some old Super Mystère BIIs. The Syrian and Egyptian air forces had over 850 planes, by contrast.

Now, in 1980, the Israelis had close to 650 planes: Skyhawk A-4, Phantoms, Israeli-made Kfir C-2s, F-15s and F-16s. The ratio between the Israelis and their adversaries was 1:1.7 as compared to 1:2.5 in 1973. Most of Israel's warplanes were more sophisticated and better equipped than those of the other air forces in the Middle East.

This, however, was not the only change. The military experts found nine areas of weakness which undermined the performance of the Israeli Air Force in 1973. By 1980, according to foreign press reports, they had corrected most of them, thus creating a more efficient and stronger war machine – one of the best in the world.

The main weaknesses of the air force in 1973, as indicated in the American press, were considered to be:

(1) Lack of effective battle management centres, which prevented co-ordination of flight of planes over the two fronts.

(2) Reconnaissance was slow and inefficient. Israel did not have the ability to process the information obtained, in real time, or at least near real time.

(3) Lack of ECM (electronic counter-measure) equipment and training. The war in 1973 was more electronic than any before, but the Israeli pilots were not sufficiently trained for such a battle.

(4) Air force pilots were trained mainly in air defence and dog-fights. Most of the combat missions were, however, attacks against targets protected by heavy anti-aircraft defence.

(5) Co-ordination between the air force and the army was poor. Inadequate communications, as well as lack of intermediate command level and liaison structure and training, denied full support of the air force to the army units at a tactical level.

(6) Central air-to-air management was not effective enough.

Many battles were allowed to develop with minimal central control and fighter allocation.

(7) The IAF had no ability at all in a combined battle of helicopters, artillery and missiles due to lack of training.

(8) Only limited training was available at all levels for long-range strike planning and executive.

(9) Lack of effective co-ordination between ground-to-air defence and air-to-air defence.

The expansion of Israeli air power 1967–81

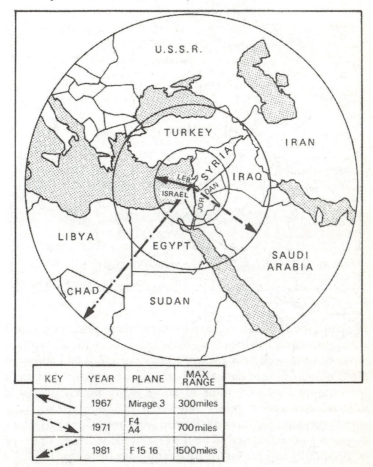

KEY	YEAR	PLANE	MAX RANGE
←	1967	Mirage 3	300 miles
⇢	1971	F4 A4	700 miles
←··	1981	F 15 16	1500 miles

Potential of F-15s and F-16s • Action radius for bombing mission (1981)

By 1980, the IAF had overcome most of these problems. It had effective central battle management capabilities for all types of mission; improved near real-time reconnaissance and ability to process and transmit data rapidly to all its command centres; it was equipped with the most advanced ECM, mostly produced in Israel itself and its pilots were better operating the sophisticated equipment; it was now trained with first priority to attack missions and considered to be the best in the world in this type of combat; it had improved its liaison with the army and navy and its central air battle management for air-to-air combat, as well as its combination and ability to operate helicopters together with ground armed forces.

Special attention was given to training in long-range strike missions. The Israelis, following the 1973 war, acquired the most advanced US fighter bombers, the F-15 and F-16, two of the 'hottest' combat planes in existence. Together with the new and very sophisticated 'Hawkeye' E-2C, which was among other things specially planned for co-ordination of such missions, bombing the Iraqi reactor near Baghdad was a difficult but not impossible mission for the Israelis. The military planners of the raid knew that the problem was not a military one. They were sure that the Israeli pilots could carry out the mission perfectly. The question was of course more a political one: getting the green light for the destruction of the reactor.

The mission against the Iraqi reactor could have been carried out by any of the major Israeli fighter-bombers, the A-4, the F-4E, the Kfir C-2, the F-15 or the F-16. The extreme range involved in the raid would have forced the team planning the raid to use air refuelling with some of the warplanes (i.e. the A-4 or Kfir C-2) probably soon after their take-off, which would have added some complications to their plan and might have led to a discovery of unusual activity on the radar screens of Jordan or Saudi Arabia, or on the way back, which might have made them vulnerable to interception either by Iraq or Jordan, requiring much longer air cover from Israeli fighters for both the returning aircraft and the bombers. It was therefore decided to avoid refuelling the attacking aircraft if possible, and the choice was thus limited to three possible aircraft – the Phantom F-4E, the Eagle F-15 and the Fighting Falcon F-16. Each of these could reach the nuclear research base in Baghdad but they would have to carry an extra load of fuel and drastically reduce their bomb load.

After a short debate it was decided to choose the F-16 Fighting Falcon,[1] produced by General Dynamics in Fort Worth, Texas, and the F-15 Eagle, produced by McDonald Douglas in St Louis, Missouri – the newest and most advanced fighter aircraft in the world. The choice fell on these two aircraft for many reasons. They were equipped with the most advanced navigational systems in the Israeli arsenal; they had a longer range than the F-4E, in particular when carrying additional fuel tanks, and they could carry heavier loads. The F-4E, while it had a Mach 2 supersonic fighter bomber, was a heavier plane which carried a smaller payload for a shorter distance and whose engines released a heavy trail of black smoke making interception and discovery much easier. Furthermore, the F-4 was a two-seater fighter bomber (i.e. pilot and navigator), which would have required letting even more people into the secret operation, and of course the fewer who knew about it, the better. But, above all, the better navigational aids of the F-15s and F-16s would allow them to fly closer to the ground, still pin-point the target, attack it and fly out faster than any other plane in operation in the world. Their greater speed and manoeuvrability were the best assurance that they would be able to attack the target as fast as possible and disappear with a much smaller chance of being intercepted by either Iraqi or Jordanian aircraft on their way home. The speed and small size of the F-16 made it the ideal aircraft to bomb the Iraqi reactor, and the F-15s were chosen to cover and protect the attacking F-16s from above. In theory the roles could have been reversed and the F-16s could cover the F-15s attacking the reactor, but the smaller size of the F-16 made them much less vulnerable to anti-aircraft fire from the ground than the two-engined F-15.

Under conditions of total surprise the Iraqi defences of the atomic reactor had practically no chance to intercept or shoot down the attacking F-16s, assuming that the Iraqi anti-aircraft teams (using the Soviet-built anti-aircraft guns ZSU-23-4 and the anti-aircraft missiles the SAM-2, SAM-3, SAM-6, SAM-9 or the French Crotale) defending the reactor would be much too slow to react. While the minutes must have seemed like forever for the attacking Israeli pilots, two minutes are nothing for defenders facing an out-of-the-blue attack.

Even had the Iraqis been partly alerted, the Israeli F-15s covering the bombing attack of the F-16s below probably carried specially designed electronic counter-measures to jam the radar controls of the SAM-6 and SAM-9 batteries as well as the semi-active receiving sensors at the head of the missiles themselves. The Israelis had captured a few samples of the SAM-6 missiles and radar during the Yom Kippur War and it seems that the seven years that had passed since then were certainly adequate to design counter-measures. Moreover, only a week before the raid, the IAF had destroyed a SAM-9 Libyan missile battery near Beirut, demonstrating that it had developed effective counter-measures to divert the enemy from the aircraft (hot-air balloons were released by the attacking aircraft and attracted the infra-red heat-detecting SAM-9 missiles). The same could be true for the more limited range and performance of the French Crotale anti-aircraft missiles. The most serious threat therefore for the Israelis was the Soviet anti-aircraft guns, the ZSU-23-4 and the Iraqi interceptors, should they be fast enough to react in time.

As far as the danger from the Iraqi interceptors was concerned, even if the Iraqi pilots could react as soon as the target was bombed, the F-16s and the F-15s were faster and could get away before the MiG-23s or 21s could even approach them. Even had the Iraqi Air Force been warned in advance – i.e. had the Israelis been discovered on the radar, which was highly unlikely given their low-profile flight – the cover supplied by the F-15s with their longer-range combination Sparrow missiles, Sidewinders and an advanced version of the Israeli-made Shafrir Mk III (Python) air-to-air missile gave the Iraqi interceptors a minimal chance to make contact with the Israeli F-16s. Furthermore, the much greater experience of the Israeli fighter pilots selected for their mission would have made an even greater difference than the superior performance of the American-made fighter aircraft and air-to-air missiles.

The Iraqi pilots were certainly much less experienced than the Israeli pilots. The combination of surprise and superior equipment and experience could not be beaten. Nevertheless, the Israeli planners did their best to ensure the success of the raid, acting as if they were attacking a fully alert and effective enemy that could and would fight back.

To achieve *complete surprise*, which was the best way to guarantee a clean operation with no loss of aircraft, certain conditions had to be met; namely, total secrecy in the planning of the operation and the choice of a flight course in which the planes would not be detected by the radar of any hostile observer who could warn the Iraqis.

Complete secrecy is relatively easy to achieve under the tight security conditions in Israel, as is the intimate familiarity of the participants with each other in such a small country.

The carefully selected pilots (fewer than a dozen were selected for the team for the mission, although only eight participated in the raid itself) were not informed about the nature of the mission. The only pilots who knew the exact target of their intensive training were the two flight commanders, Lieutenant-Colonels Zeev Raz and Amir Nahumi, and the Commander of the Ramat David IAF base, Colonel Yiftah Spector, who was also the commander of the IAF F-16 wing. Even they did not know the date of the mission, which was disclosed to them only a day before it actually took place. Needless to say, they were not allowed to talk about the mission to their families or any other unauthorized person.

Despite all the efforts to contain the secret of the operation within a limited circle of participants there were some unplanned leaks. Fortunately, all such leaks were kept within a circle of trusted people. Some of those who were informed had only a general idea of the planning of the operation, while others had specific knowledge of the date of the operation. Among those who knew of the operation in advance was former Defence Minister Ezer Weizman, now a political adversary of Begin. Weizman, a former hawk and since the late 1970s a convinced dove, tried to arouse support against the operation from the opposition leaders. He gave information on the raid to the leader of the Opposition, former Prime Minister Shimon Peres,[2] who in turn discussed the planned raid with former Prime Minister and Chief of Staff Yitzhak Rabin, former Chief of Staff Mordechai ('Mota') Gur, former Foreign Minister Abba Eban and other senior members of the opposition party. Information on the planned raid also reached a reporter close to Weizman and a former TV correspondent and a close aide of Shimon Peres.

The leaks caused considerable concern to Prime Minister Begin and his close aids. As a result it was decided to delay the attack a least twice, once (on 10 May) after the pilots and Air Force had already been given the green light to go ahead. Despite the fact that the opposition leaders, in the midst of a tough election campaign, were strongly against the raid on political, diplomatic and military grounds – they did not leak the information outside.[3]

Because of delays in the operation caused by these leaks Begin put the government decision on the specific date of the raid not in the hands of the permanent regular cabinet committee on defence and foreign affairs, but in the hands of a special sub-committee which included only himself, Foreign Minister Shamir and IDF Chief of Staff Raphael Eitan (the so-called Committee of Three).[4] This committee, in collaboration with the Chief of Staff later decided on the *final* date of the raid – 7 June 1981. This action improved the secrecy surrounding the timing of the operation itself, but even so the opposition leaders learned of the raid some eight hours in advance and had enough time to meet and discuss the impact the raid might have on the forthcoming election *before* it took place!

It can be estimated that at least 80–100 people knew in advance of the intention to destroy the Iraqi nuclear reactor at some time and that a smaller number had knowledge of the precise day in advance once it was finally decided. So far as secrecy was necessary to achieve surprise, it is clear that, despite the internal haemorrhage of secrets, no information fell into adverse hands.

But the achievement of total surprise also depended on the meticulous planning of the operation itself. The aircraft (14 in all) had to approach the target without being detected at all...

NOTES

1. By 1981 the F-16 had been ordered or purchased by the following countries: Belgium (116), Denmark (58), the Netherlands (102), Norway (72), as well as the US (over 2,000), Iran (160 – the order for these was cancelled following the Khomeini revolution in Iran in 1979). In 1977 Israel ordered an initial 75 F-16s. Ironically, as a result of the cancellation of the Iranian order, the IAF was able to obtain the aircraft originally built for Iran in Fort Worth, Texas and took delivery of the first F-16s two years ahead of the planned schedule. The first was delivered to Israel on 31 January 1980. Had it not been for the Iranian Muslim revolution the IAF could still have carried out the mission against the Iraqi nuclear reactor, but with greater difficulties and at a higher risk. (The raid would then probably have been carried out by a combination of F-15s and F-4s or by F-15s only, acting as both air cover and air-to-ground bombers.) A double irony is of course that in 1979 the Iranians could not have predicted their war with Iraq and that the aircraft were in fact delivered into the hands of another of Iraq's adversaries. The Israeli attack on the Iraqi nuclear reactor probably relieved Iran of a considerable amount of pressure just as it did Israel. From this point of view the Iranians could not (despite their faint protests

TWO MINUTES OVER BAGHDAD

against Israel) have been more pleased. Other F-16s were to be sold to Egypt (40 + 40), to Venezuela and in all likelihood to many other countries as well. It must be mentioned that the brilliant execution of the Israeli Air Force in the Iraqi nuclear raid was probably the best possible advertisement for US aircraft manufacturers (General Dynamics and McDonald Douglas). The Israelis had thus done a great service to US aircraft manufacturers in a highly competitive market. They did in fact advertise American-made fighters – in the same way as they used to advertise the Mirage III for the French. (The Mirage III had practically no customers until Israel achieved such dramatic success with its Mirage IIIs during the 1967 Six Day War.) No wonder therefore that the French aircraft industry was no less worried about the brilliant Israeli performance with the F-16 than were the Arabs and Iraqis. The Israelis thereafter preferred US to French aircraft and rejected a French offer either to purchase or locally produce the Mirage F-1. The General Dynamics Corporation was then ready to come out with a cheaper export version of the F-16 equipped with a smaller power plant, the Pratt and Whitney J-79.

2. Peres was generally briefed on the intention to destroy the Iraqi reactor by Prime Minister Begin himself in December 1980 but did not receive any concrete information on the plans. Later, in May and in June, Weizman and other sources within the army gave Peres advance knowledge of the D-Day and H-Hour itself. Peres then wrote and sent on 9 May – a day before the day due for the attack – an urgent letter to Begin asking him to cancel or delay the raid. As a result of this breach of secrecy premier Begin and the Chief of Staff decided to delay the raid.

3. It must be remembered that in 1981 those who were now the opposition leaders had been for close to 30 years responsible for all the decisions and policies concerning Israeli security and military policies and therefore had their own connections and close contact with senior officers of the Israeli Army, many of whom were closely affiliated with their party and who had a great deal of sympathy for their cause. As a result it was extremely difficult to keep even the most classified state secrets from the leaders of the opposition.

4. Begin, who was a shrewd and experienced politician, decided to move the decision concerning the timing of the raid to the 'Committee of Three' not only in order to improve secrecy but also to confine it to a group which had similar opinions to his own – and who would *not* hesitate to carry the decision through. The larger cabinet committee on Defence and Foreign Affairs was divided on the decision itself and a number of the religious party ministers as well as Yigael Yadin, the Deputy Prime Minister, raised considerable objections to the timing, if not the idea, of the raid.

15

Operation Babylon:
The Approach Route

The planning of the approach route to the target was of the greatest importance. The Middle East was then in a continual state of warfare and therefore in a relatively permanent state of high alert. As a result the area was saturated by overlapping radar stations covering almost all possible directions.

During the early stages of the war with Iran, the Iraqis preferred to defend their airfields by adopting a Soviet system (also used over North Vietnam) in which approaching enemy aircraft were intercepted as far as possible from their targets and close to the border. Later on, with the growing success of the Iranian low-level air attacks, which the Iraqis failed to intercept, they changed their anti-aircraft defences and concentrated on heavier anti-aircraft fire and interception efforts close to their major installations. This change in tactics led to a considerable strengthening of air defences around the Iraqi nuclear reactor. The Soviet type of forward air defence made it easier to identify a friend or foe and was better where radar and ground control was weak.

Despite the fact that the Iraqis had participated in no fewer than three wars against Israel, the Israelis still knew relatively little about them (in terms of their performance on the battlefield, command, initiative, and so on). The Iraqi difficulties in their war against Iran seemed to indicate that their capabilities had probably been grossly overestimated by Israeli intelligence.

Nevertheless a great deal of attention was invested in planning and covering up the approach of the warplanes to their target. This was probably achieved in five mutually overlapping ways. The first was to choose a course of flight in between

Radar coverage on Israel's eastern front

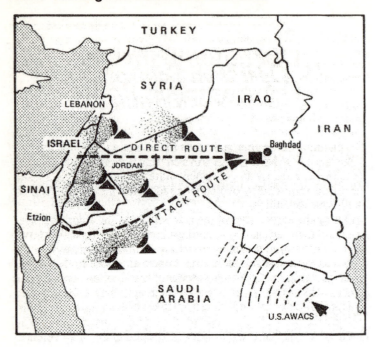

enemy radars so that the aircraft would not be detected; the
second was to fly as low as possible, so that even if the aircraft
were to fly through an area normally covered by radar they
would be *below* the detecting range and level of the radars; the
third was the strict maintenance of radio silence; fourth, the
blinding of the enemy's radars or, by what is known as ECM or
Electronic Counter Measures (Electronic Warfare), by presenting a different image (a number of aircraft flying in certain formations can appear as one large aircraft) or by presenting no
radar image at all on the enemy's radar screen (by the use of
special paints that do not reflect radar waves; by the use of
radar echoes that cancel the echoes returning from the aircraft;
or by jamming or other 'stealth' technologies); fifth and finally,
if the planes were detected in mid-flight the pilots could still
avoid identification by direct deception – by pretending that
they were Jordanian or Saudi pilots on a training mission, by

not using clear identification marks and by the passive means of camouflage.

I. The IAF planning team could certainly not choose the straightest and most direct way to Baghdad. The shortest way over southern Syria and northern Jordan was closely watched by both the Syrians and Jordanians – above all the former, who were in the midst of the unresolved Syrian–Israeli Bekkah missile crisis following the Syrian advance of SAM-6 anti-aircraft missiles into eastern Lebanon. This crisis was far from being resolved and the US Special Ambassador, Philip Habib, was still continuing his shuttle diplomacy between Damascus, Beirut, Jerusalem and Riad. In the meantime the Israelis continued their intensified air operations over the Lebanon against the PLO, and the Syrians could be expected to be on special alert – given Begin's promise to attack the Syrian missile sites in the Bekkah (and possibly elsewhere). The Syrians therefore kept a close radar watch on their southern border. The Jordanians also had a full-range radar coverage on their northern border. The only choice, therefore, was to take the longer but safer southern route to the target. Since southern Jordan also had an almost completely foolproof radar coverage, the best southern route was possibly as far south as possible over Jordanian or Saudi territory.

We now know that the Israeli aircraft took off on their flight to Baghdad from the large Etzion base near Eilat (one of the largest and most modern military air bases in the world). This air base is 15 miles (at the most) from the Jordanian border and under continual radar and possibly also optical surveillance. Unless the planes' departure could be covered by counter-electronic measures blinding the Jordanian radars, they would have to fly extremely low in order to avoid detection.[1]

II. The second and complementary way to avoid detection was by flying at tree-top level close to the ground, well under the normal detection level of ground stations. (Airborne radars such as the AWACS Boeing E-3 or the Hawkeye E-2 could also detect low-flying aircraft even against complex ground clutter.) In all probability the Israelis flew a great deal of the flight course to Iraq at 30–60 feet, but never more than 200 feet, depending on the terrain. In fact, they can be said to have followed the terrain contour as efficiently and at as low an altitude as possible.

Navigation and the flight itself put an extremely heavy pressure and workload on the pilots and required great skill, cool nerves and endurance. Under any normal flight conditions such a low-altitude flight is considered extremely dangerous. However, al Israeli pilots are trained to fly extremely low, since it is well known that this is their best defence against fighter interception and anti-aircraft fire. The two dozen or so pilots who trained for Operational Babylon probably refined their low-level flight techniques and low-level navigational expertise against the difficult-to-navigate desert background.

This low-level flight course not only created difficulties in navigation but drastically shortened the range of the aircraft: low-level flying involves greater 'friction', the primary cause of higher fuel consumption. To overcome this range reduction the amount of fuel available to the attacking aircraft would have to be increased and this could be done in two ways.

Firstly, by refuelling soon after take-off (when the highest proportion of fuel is consumed) or en route to the target – both of which are easy but considerably increase the chances of being detected: refuelling 14 or so planes takes a long time and at least four to six refuelling aircraft (depending on the number of aircraft that can simultaneously be refuelled by each tanker aircraft).

The second option is to add disposable fuel tanks to each aircraft. These will often more than double the range but will automatically halve the amount of ammunition payload each aircraft will be able to carry. Doubling the number of aircraft would therefore be necessary to drop the bombs required to destroy the target.

Refuelling on the way back was out of the question, for two reasons. If difficulties arose in refuelling on the way back, the aircraft would not make it back home. Secondly, assuming that enemy intercepting aircraft took after the attacking aircraft, refuelling under attack would be impossible. Furthermore the tanks are big and slow, and therefore highly vulnerable to enemy interceptors.

In the best tradition of simplifying the operation as much as

possible the Israelis decided to eliminate the refuelling procedures in the air at *any* stage of the raid and extended the range
of the attacking aircraft by adding extra fuel tanks to each aircraft. This of course meant that the number of planes participating in the raid had to be increased.

III. In addition to careful attention to the approach to the target, the aircraft themselves (in particular the F-15s but possibly
other special intelligence aircraft) were equipped with electronic counter-measures to blind or deceive the enemy's radar.
Nothing is known about the equipment: but it can be assumed
that much of it would have been made in Israel. Israeli sophis-
tication in this most secret type of warfare is well known and is
indicated by what little the Israelis choose to show at international air show exhibitions or on a commercial basis. In addition to the Israeli-produced equipment, the Israelis have
obtained a large variety of American counter-electronic equipment. Judging by the results, the equipment used was highly
successful and the aircraft were not detected on the way to the
target. As we now know the raid came as a total surprise, not
only to the Iraqis but also the Americans, Jordanians and
Saudis.

The stationing of the American Boeing AWEACS 3A in
Saudi Arabia following the revolution in Iran and the Iran–Iraq
war to protect Saudi air space certainly gave the Israelis good
reason to worry. It is not known whether the Israelis jammed or
deceived by presenting the wrong image on the AWACS radar
screen (it was rumoured that the Israeli aircraft flew in a tight
formation which projects on a radar screen an image of *one*
large aircraft such as a Boeing 747) or whether they used any
other technology to project false images – or simply used equipment to destroy the emanation or reception of any radar signals
completely. One way or another the AWACS did not discover
the approach *or* withdrawal of the Israeli aircraft. The simplest
explanation is probably that the AWACS were flying too far
away to the south-east, concentrating on the north-eastern part
of the Persian Gulf or the Shatt al Arab, to discover the Israelis.

In addition the Israelis, who always operated under the
assumption that they were being closely watched by US and
Soviet satellites from above, took extra precautions to avoid

any such observation. This means that the most important activities and special preparations would have taken place either underground or in closed hangars. All activity observed by satellites would have either been unimportant, and not indicative of what operations were being planned, or been used for deception. American intelligence has been unjustifiably blamed for failing to learn or anticipate the raid. This, however, would have been impossible. Americans put too much emphasis on technological intelligence (i.e. satellites, electronic snooping etc.), which has very clear limitations. Knowledge on such an operation can only be obtained by what is called HUMINT – or human intelligence. The spy from within.

IV and V. Detection en route to the target could also be avoided by maintaining radio silence and, if discovered by any hostile radar or air controller, by answering in Arabic (or English). There were rumours immediately following the raid that an inquisitive radar operator in Saudi Arabia who had discovered the planes on the way to the target was responded to in Arabic, that the Israelis used the Royal Jordanian call signs and frequencies, and that the penetrating Israeli pilots pretended to be Jordanian Air Force pilots on a training exercise. (Such a report appeared in the reputable *Aviation Week and Space Technology* of 15 June 1981, p. 32.) But it is highly doubtful that such an incident ever took place. Such rumours always appear after such operations and are normally to be discounted as mere fabrications of the fertile cloak-and-dagger minds of journalists.

In reality, it appears that the Israeli pilots, so well rehearsed for the operation, maintained total radio silence both on the way to the target and on the way back. The evidence for this lies in the statement of one of the pilots interviewed after the raid, who said that he had been very worried on the way back not knowing what had happened to the other pilots. This could mean two things. Firstly, that the pilots kept radio silence either for the total operation or at least on the way back, and, secondly, that they did not maintain visual contact on the way back, and that, to make interception more difficult, they each flew back to Israel over Jordanian territory (which is the shortest possible route) by different routes.

1: A hot refuelling of Major Yadlin's F-16 a couple of minutes before taking off on the mission.

2: The first quadruple ready to take off at Etzion airbase. From right to left: Lieutenant-Colonel Zeev Raz, Major Amos Yadlin, Major Dubi, and Major Hagai.

3: The reactor, as seen by the VTR camera of an F-16 pilot, before the explosion of the first bombs.

4: The reactor, as seen by the VTR camera, after the explosion of the first bombs.

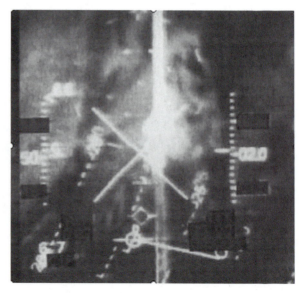

5: The pilots and the planner. A historic picture of the eight F-16 pilots that bombed the reactor and the planner of the operation, taken at Etzion airbase, immediately after the pilots had returned from their mission. Sitting on the right, Lieutenant-Colonel Zeev Raz, the operation's commander; on his right, his No. 2, Major Amos Yadlin. Second row (covered faces), on the right Major Dubi; on his right Major Hagai. Third row, on the right (holding fingers) Lieutenant-Colonel Amir Nahumi; on his right, his No. 2, Colonel Yiftah Spector. Standing, on the right, Major Relik Shafir; on his right, Lieutenant Ilan Ramon. Standing on their left, Colonel Aviem Sella.

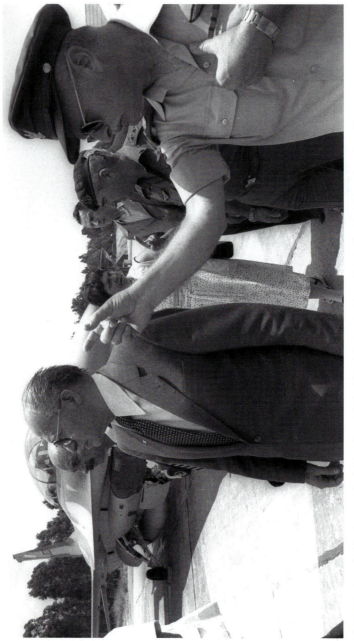

6: PM Begin and IAF Commander Major-General David Ivri during a visit to Ramat David airbase after the raid.

7. Chief of Staff Raphael Eitan and PM Begin.

8. Deputy PM Yigael Yadin, PM Menachem Begin and IAF Commander David Ivri during the same visit to Ramat David airbase.

9. An IAF Officer briefs government ministers about the raid during the visit to Ramat David airbase.

10. Press conference after the raid. From left to right: Chief of Staff Eitan, IAF Commander Ivri and AMAN's director, Major-General Saguy.

11. IAF Commander receives a citation from PM Begin for Operation Opera.

The Israeli planners, then, did the best they could to achieve total surprise over the target area so as to avoid any anti-aircraft fire or the intervention of Iraqi interceptors en route to the target.

They were helped by other factors which directed attention away from the possibility of such an attack. The first was the Iraqi–Iranian war, which must have directed most of the Iraqi military and intelligence efforts to the east towards Iran and not to the west towards Israel. This was probably the case both in terms of Iraqi perception and attention and in terms of their radar surveillance interceptor fighter cover.[2] The Iraqis also probably assumed that any attack would occur on a much smaller scale (of two or at most four attacking aircraft).

Since in the past three wars with Iraq the Israeli Air Force had never attacked any Iraqi targets in the vicinity of Baghdad the Iraqis probably did not see such an attack as realistically possible. In this context it must be remembered that Iraq had actively participated in and declared war against Israel in 1948, 1967 and 1973 and had never signed an armistice or ceasefire agreement with Israel. The two countries were therefore tech-nically in a permanent state of war with each other and there-fore the Israeli's attack on Iraq cannot be considered an illegal act according to international law. In 1967 Iraqi long-range Soviet-made TU-16 bombers attacked the Israeli city of Netanya on the Mediterranean coast. One of the two Iraqi bombers was shot down en route back home. The Israelis them-selves had never attacked any targets in Iraq before, with the exception of an attack on Iraqi military airfield H-3 halfway between Israel and Baghdad. At that time the attack on H-3 was at the most extreme range of the aircraft then available to the Israeli Air Force.

The second major distraction that may have dulled Iraqi attention to the possibility of an Israeli air attack on their nuclear reactor was the Israeli–Syrian missile crisis, which seemed to indicate that Israel was fully preoccupied with the situation to its north and not to the east with Iraq. Indeed, later on, following the successful raid on the Iraqi nuclear reactor, Begin – who was sharply criticized during the ongoing Israeli election campaign for his clumsy handling and the initiation of the missile crisis – claimed in public that the missile crisis was nothing but a ruse to deflect attention from the planned attack on the Iraqi reactor. Begin was probably trying either to cash in on the success of the raid on Iraq and tell the voters how smart he was, or else he might have been trying to defuse the Israeli–Syrian missile crisis by showing that it was merely a sideshow and not Israel's major concern. One way or another this explanation presented by Begin after the event failed to impress anyone and was quickly withdrawn.

Additional diversionary moves were probably the Iraqi perception that the Israelis were unlikely to attack the reactor in the midst of their election campaign, and that they would not attack the reactor before the work on the reactor had been completed.

The combination of the detailed preparation for the attack combined with the diversionary background noises were to create the ideal conditions for a successful surprise attack on the reactor.

NOTES

1. The planes were to take off from Etzion at about 3.00 Israeli time (i.e. in broad daylight) on their two-hour flight to the target. 7 June was on the eve of the Jewish Shavouth holiday in which normal military activity in Israel could be expected to be considerably reduced. Any Jordanian observers familiar with Jewish holidays should have therefore noticed the unusual activity taking place at Etzion.
2. The Iraqi reactor had been slightly damaged by two Iranian Phantom F-4s on 30 September 1980. Since that attack the air war between Iran and Iraq had been considerably reduced while the lack of Iranian aircraft and spare parts made a large-scale attack highly improbable.

16

Operation Babylon:
A Choice of Weapons

The flight approach was planned to be at tree-top level. The attacking aircraft were to fly in two groups. The bombing group included eight Fighting Falcon F-16 single-seat single-engine fighter bombers. The second included six F-15 Eagles, a single-seat, two-engined, all-weather air-superiority fighter serving as cover for the bombing F-16s.

Once the aircraft approached the target (perhaps as far away as 40 miles from the target) the F-15 group were to fly much higher to cover the approaching F-16s from above. The F-15s would also carry advanced counter-electronic measures or jamming pads – to neutralize the radar and guidance of the SAM-6 anti-aircraft batteries and the radar of the ZSU-23-4 anti-aircraft guns. In addition, they were also to cover anti-radiation air-to-ground missiles, such as the Shrike missile, that could also be used to neutralize the anti-aircraft defences of the reactor. But above all the F-15 was to carry a large number of air-to-air missiles, probably a combination of the Israeli-made Shafrir missile (possibly an advanced second- or third-generation version called 'Python') as well as US-made Sidewinders AIM-9 and the longer-range Sparrows AIM-7.

The F-16s in the meantime were to continue for a while to fly below, gradually elevate to 1,500–2,000 feet towards the target itself and then, just above the target, to dive down again almost to tree-top level to secure *direct* hits on the target.

The approach was such that the F-16s came first, flying lower and lower, while the F-15s covered them. Thus, the faster F-15s would appear at the same time over the target as the F-16s – at a different height. Immediately following the attack the F-16s would turn and quickly climb to meet the waiting F-15s circling above.

During the withdrawal phase home, the structure of the groups would again change. This time the F-15s and F-16s would combine in pairs – each pair taking a slightly different course home to make interception (should the Iraqis attempt one) more difficult. The route back, unlike the circumspect route towards the target, would be as high and as direct as possible in order to conserve fuel. All in all the flight would take close to four hours, with the aircraft spending two and a half hours on course to the target, two minutes over the target, and about an hour and a half on the flight back to their bases.

Detailed but undiscovered rescue arrangements had been made in case any of the pilots had to bail out. No information concerning this emergency rescue operation has been discovered, but it was certainly very elaborate and probably involved bearer aircraft (such as the Lockheed Hercules C-130, which can land on short and primitive runways and can take off from very short runways, with the assistance of rockets; there are also techniques by which a C-130 can rescue a stranded pilot from the ground without landing). As with all such eventualities, detailed arrangements were made for signalling and communicating between the pilots and rescue planes, meeting points and the like.

Other rescue combinations could have also included helicopters that could take off from the C-130s after they had landed and proceed to more difficult types of terrain where the C-130s could not land. In all probability a few C-130s were in the air (or at least on special alert), all the time, possibly with fighters to give them cover. The prospects of bailing out over Iraq certainly did not make any of the Israeli pilots any happier: if any of them were captured by the Iraqis they stood almost no chance of ever returning home.

Finally, if the raid were to succeed and all the Israeli aircraft returned, it would still be necessary to put the IAF on alert for a few days against the possibility of a hastily planned Iraqi retaliatory raid.

The choice of weapons or bombs to be dropped on the target was of course crucial. The attacking aircraft were taking a very high risk on their approach to the target and, should they fail to destroy the nuclear reactor in one or, at the most, two quick passes over the reactor, they would have *no* second chance. The reason was obvious: following a first unsuccessful large-scale attack the Iraqis would certainly strengthen their anti-aircraft defences even further, in particular radar coverage.

The chance of attacking the reactor by achieving total surprise would then be dismissed and any further attempt to attack the target from the air would involve much heavier costs. The attacking aircraft had therefore to carry enough extra capacity to ensure the destruction of the target, even if some of the bomb-carrying aircraft did not make it.

Having the example of the failure of the American rescue mission in April 1980 in the Iranian desert (mainly as a result of not taking enough helicopters, should some of them be damaged in action), the Israelis decided to ensure the success of the raid by arming the attacking force with a surplus of weapons. Thus if only seven tons of bombs (or approximately 15,000lb of TNT) were sufficient to destroy the target, the attacking aircraft would carry no less than 15 tons (or 32,000lb).

The IAF in 1981 had in its arsenal some of the most sophisticated American and Israeli-made stand-off[1] precision guided munitions (or PGMs),[2] such as the GBU 15 electro-optical (EO) modular glide weapon system – a regular MK84 iron 'dumb' 2,000lb bomb to which a set of wings as well as television guidance and homing devices are added – and the AGM 62A Walleye air-to-surface missile, another gliding bomb of 850lb with high explosives (another and later model of this type of bomb is the Walleye II MK5 which carries 2,000lb of high explosives), electro-optically guided and designed primarily to hit semi-hard targets such as bridges, air-base facilities and strips. Other and smaller guided precision missiles in the Israeli arsenal were the AGM 12 Bullseye and the Maverick AGM-65 air-to-surface missile.

Any of these weapons could have caused serious damage to the Iraqi reactor, particularly the GBU 15 and the Walleye weapon system. The planning team of the IAF decided not to choose any of these weapon systems in their desire to keep everything in the raid as simple as possible. Indeed, while precision-guided munitions (PGMs) are under ideal conditions the most precise to operate, they require special circumstances that are not always easy to obtain under battlefield conditions. They require, for example, operation from a minimum height; the use of an aircraft with two operators rather than one (one to operate the guidance system of the weapon and one to fly the aircraft); certain weather conditions; a stabilized pattern of flight for 20 or more seconds; and finally, they have many electronic parts – electronic sensors, wings, rocket engines – all of which increase the chance that something may not work and reduce the reliability of the bombs. Moreover, unlike free-fall bombs or ballistically fixed weapons, PGMs can *always* be subject to interference, jamming and a variety of counter-measures.

All these requirements are difficult to meet in a low-level surprise attack on a heavily defended target. Therefore, the planners of the operation chose the more traditional, conventional type of large iron 'dumb' bombs. The bomb chosen was probably the American-made MK84 2,000lb (907kg) high-explosive conventional iron, dumb bomb (or a similar Israeli-made bomb). This was highly reliable, has been tested in numerous operations and had never failed. It carried enough high explosive to cause serious damage to some of the hardest targets. To have the desired impact, i.e. destroy the target, it *must* hit the target right on dead centre, otherwise, depending on the distance by which it missed the target, its impact would be negligible. This is true for all conventional bombs that are target point bombs – i.e. intended against *specific* targets which must be hit and *not* area targets such as a spread group of attacking tanks, infantry, etc. ᴏ ᴿ ᴄ ι ᴛ ι ᴇ ѕ

The ability of conventional munitions to destroy even the strongest built nuclear reactor has been noted for example by Bennett Ramberg (*Destruction of Nuclear Energy Facilities in War*, chapter 2), where he suggests:

> The energy release of these [conventional] munitions is a function of their composition and the shaping of the charge to perform the specific tasks. A 100lb general-purpose dumb bomb can penetrate more than 2ft of concrete and 4m of steel. Since its power is proportional to its size, its 2,000lb counterpart can pierce more than 11ft of concrete and up to 15m of steel.

Heavy, shaped charges are even more effective. An 800kg (1,700lb) conical-shaped munition 89cm in diameter and 1m long with a steel liner can penetrate 10m of concrete ...

Each of the MK84 bombs used by the Israelis was powerful enough to destroy the reactor, which certainly was not thicker than 11 feet of concrete.

The advantage of this type of bombs is that they can be dropped on the target (unlike most precision-guided bombs) from a very low height. The attacking Israeli warplanes had therefore to be absolutely sure that they would all score *direct* hits on the targets. This was achieved by an intense training programme, by exact navigation right to the target, by flying from tree-top level to a height of over 2,000ft, and finally by diving and releasing the bombs at the centre of the target from as low as 50–100ft – which would ensure perfect hits. Later, following the raid, US satellite photographs showed the hits on the Iraqi nuclear reactor to have been so precise that American intelligence officers were convinced that the Israelis had used precision-guided munition. What the American intelligence analysts did not apparently know is that Israeli pilots usually achieve such precision by bombing their targets from much lower than would normally be considered safe for American pilots.

The F-16 could, when the intended fuel capacity was reduced, carry up to 15,200lb (or 6,895kg) against short-range targets or with full internal fuel, up to 12,000lb (or 5,443kg) to a larger range. The very long range of the operation had forced the planners to add an extra large amount of fuel to the attacking aircraft. This in fact meant that each fighter bomber had to carry a heavier load of fuel than bombs. Each F-16 therefore carried only 2 MK84 2,000lb bombs. In all, the eight F-16s carried 16 bombs, a total weight of 32,000lb of high explosives (or a total of 14,512kg or 14.5 metric tons). In all probability two or four well-aimed bombs could have completely destroyed the Iraqi reactor. The Israeli planning team wanted to be extra sure and as a precaution at least doubled the number of aircraft and bombs.

NOTES

1. *Stand-off* weapons are weapons that can be released or fired at their targets outside the anti-aircraft defence perimeter. They can be released from distances of 8–10 miles away and make their way to the target either by powerless gliding or assisted by small rockets. They can be guided directly to the centre of their target by towing a combination of laser energy, radio control, electro-optical guidance (or television guidance) FLIR (forward-looking infra-red), which homes on the extra heat emitted by the target or combinations of the above.

2. Precision-guided munitions or PGMs are weapons that are either directed to the target by an observer who can correct their flight to the target by the use of radio, wire control and the like, or can automatically home in on the target by themselves (homing on heat or a TV image for example). They are defined as weapons that hit a target with a probability of at least 50 per cent. Although such weapons have frequently been referred to as revolutionary innovations they had in fact appeared on both the German and Allied side during World War II. ✔

Key to map opposite:

A Six Israeli F-15 Fighters and eight F-16 Fighter Bombers take off from the Sinai (Etzion) Air Base.

B The Israeli aircraft fly at tree-top level over Saudi Arabian territory, tightly grouped in two formations.

C They continue to fly at tree-top level, turning slowly north-east to Baghdad. One F-15 separates off and flies as cover, operating counter-electronic measures.

D The two formations split at this point. The F-15s climb up to a height of 12–18,000 feet to cover the attacking F-16s, while the F-16s climb to a level of 1,000–2,000 feet and dive again to tree-top level when they attack the reactor. Each of them drops two MK.84 iron bombs on the target.

E Iraqi anti-aircraft fire is ineffective and is opened only when the planes depart. Soviet and French surface-to-air SAM-6, SAM-9 and Croatle missiles are never fired. Iraqi interceptors take off too late to intercept the attacking aircraft.

F The F-16s and F-15s combine into seven pairs to make interception more difficult, and disperse on the way home. They fly the shortest possible route to base at a very high altitude to conserve fuel and to land back at base.

The Flight Course to the Target – June 7th 1981

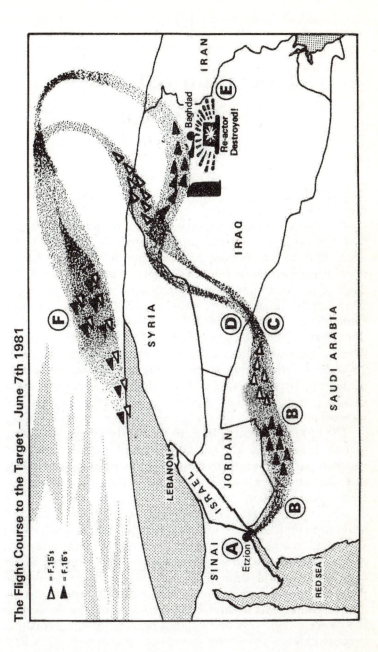

△ = F.15's
▲ = F.16's

17

Operation Babylon:
Countdown

A dozen pilots started their intensive training programme some time in October 1980. All their training was conducted under similar desert terrains. They worked hard on precision navigation, many hours of low tree-top flying (which is extremely difficult over the monotonous desert terrain) in very tight formations of eight to ten F-16s and a similar sized group of F-15s, while at the same time following a close terrain contour flight. They learned how to break away quickly under the threat of enemy fighters, and to improve the visual contact communication and the line of tight co-ordination between the pilots, which in turn would improve the co-ordination between the F-16 and F-15 pilots. They trained in breaking up the formations of aircraft, flying in pairs of F-15s and F-16s back to base – though it was most likely that they would return in one tight formation.

The formations had to learn to rely on the navigation of one or two leaders while the rest concentrated on their flight and watched their radar screens closely for any possible appearance of enemy aircraft. Others had to operate their special counter-electronic equipment.

They had to practise the approach on the target again and again until they could do it practically blindfolded. Each of the F-16s had to attack the target on its own in no more than two or four minutes in all: each one had to buzz over the target some 8–10 seconds after the other, each knowing his precise place and timing in the attack. Each had to concentrate on the target, ignore *any* anti-aircraft fire and drop the bombs right at the centre or on areas that had not been hit by the pilots that preceded him.

The training exercises were considered so vital that the Israeli Chief of Staff, Eitan, himself participated in one in order to get a first-hand idea of how such a raid worked and of the problems involved.

By the time the go-ahead for action was given and after the two or three delays in the timing of the attack, the two teams of pilots knew the drill backwards. The only thing they did not know – D-Day – was revealed to the pilots 24 hours before the attack by Colonel Yiftah Spector, the commander of the Ramat David base, who himself participated in the raid.

Colonel Aviem Sella, the chief planner of the raid, has compared the intensive and repeated training to the rehearsing of a symphony orchestra. All the pilots and fighters worked according to the same plan, just as the musicians in an orchestra work to the same score.

'After such detailed and meticulous training preparations and finesse are created', he remarked, 'you say to them "Concerto no.42 by Brahms" – and everyone plays. Everyone knows very well what music we're going to play!'

The conductor saw to it that their action was co-ordinated. No more words were needed. And in this case there was to be no audience.

18

Operation Babylon: Two Minutes over Osirak

Sunday 7 June, a beautiful clear day. The small town of Eilat, the Israeli tourist centre on the Red Sea, was overcrowded with thousands of Scandinavian, German and Israeli tourists who came perhaps to enjoy the sandy beaches of the Red Sea, before they are returned to the Egyptians as part of the Peace Treaty between the two states. This Sunday was a 'bridge day', between the Jewish Sabbath and the feast of Shavouth; it signalled in the long Jewish history in Israel of two thousand years the beginning of collecting the winter crops.

None of the tourists was aware of the special activity in the airbase of Etzion, some 20km from Eilat. For 24 hours one of the best and most modern airbases in the world had been unusually busy. It is a regular routine in Israel that most of the regular army soldiers receive the weekend off. All regular training is stopped on the Sabbath, and planes are ready to fly only in combat missions under a short alert. This particular weekend, however, all leave had been cancelled, even to take a trip to Eilat.

This was one of the measures taken by the army's Security Field Service, to eliminate any chance of leaking the big secret. For the same reason, all telephone communication lines, except for some special operation ones in the headquarters of the base, were cut off. Although only the pilots who were chosen for the mission and some other senior officers were to know about the planned raid, those who were in charge of its security kept in mind the incident five years before, during the preparations for the Entebbe raid, when it was found out only a few hours before the planes took off, that a soldier serving at the base had called his girlfriend to tell her that he would not be able to come home as promised, because 'we prepare something special for Idi Amin'.

The base was still closed late in the morning when a CH-53 helicopter landed near its headquarters. The Israeli Chief of Staff, Raphael Eitan, accompanied by Major-Generals David Ivri, the commander of the Israeli Air Force, and Yehoshua Saguy, the head of the military intelligence, and some other senior officers who had been in on the planning of the operation since its inception, came out and were taken to the main briefing hall.

Deep inside the large air-conditioned underground operations room, they were met by 14 pilots and Aviem Sella, the 32-year-old air force colonel, the brain behind the planning of the raid, and who now started the final briefing.

Everybody in the room had been primed for every detail of the plan. Each of them knew the exact flying route, the way they should take off with the heavy loads of fuel and ammunition, the flight patterns of the Eagles and Fighting Falcons, the measures taken for rescue if one of the pilots were to desert his plane, and many other small but very important details needed for the success of the daring mission. Each of them had participated in such a briefing in the past at least once. They were aware of the fact that this operation, for which they had prepared themselves so carefully, had been cancelled at the last minute at least twice, and hoped that this time the real action would begin. The atmosphere in the big neon-lit room was quiet but tense.

Outside, in the big hangars, some of them underground, hundreds of technicians were already preparing the planes for the mission. The special ECM devices in the F-15s were checked and re-checked. Air-to-air missiles were carefully fixed to the wings of the F-16s and the fighter bombers were armed with the MK84 iron bombs. Even at this stage, not one of these soldiers knew what the task was to be. They were well aware, of course, that a special mission was to be carried out but they could not guess its target. Some of them guessed that the target was the Syrian missile battery at the northern border. Others, who considered that the iron bombs were not the best device against such targets, rejected their friends' assumptions, but could not offer a better alternative.

The technical officer of each squadron, accompanied by his senior aides, personally made the last check of each plane when the pilots returned from their briefing, each carrying his crash helmet.

Some minutes before 15.00 local time, the young pilots entered their planes and the canopies were shut from above. Few of them were nervous, having trained for so long for all eventualities and the worst-possible developments. They pressed a button and the sound of roaring engines was heard all over the base. Moving forward, the long, broad runway was now visible to their eyes. Each pair of fighter bombers, loaded to full capacity, took off, using the whole length of the runway because of the heavy weight they were carrying.

The Chief of Staff of the IDF and the other generals looked up, crossing their fingers, and watched the airplanes disappear low-flying in the blue sky, toward the south-east. Their faces were tense but expressionless. They would have to wait for at least two hours before they would know whether the mission had succeeded or failed. It was agreed that the communication system would not be used – unless in an emergency situation – in order to avoid detection by enemy forces. Now, nothing was left for Eitan, Ivry and the rest of them to do, except to chain-smoke cigarettes and glance repeatedly at their watches.

The planes were by now flying over the thousands of tourists enjoying the beaches of the Red Sea. Nobody paid attention to the low-flying fighters. 'Another one of those long and boring exercise flights', was the common thought that crossed the minds of the many Israelis who were watching them, some of them IDF pilots themselves.

The flight to Osirak was uneventful, as the pilots recalled hours later. During the many monotonous hours of the training they had undertaken, each of them had faced many possible contingencies – being discovered on the way to the target, heavier than expected anti-aircraft fire, interception on the way to or back from the target by Saudi, Iraqi or Jordanian fighters, and always the possibility of some technical hitch.

Everything, however, went exactly as planned. They were flying now over the northern parts of the Saudi desert. The F-15 in the lead was navigating them to the Tammuz project, through the many radar stations positioned in this part of the region. They flew very low, about 30 to 60 feet above ground level. No word was heard in their communication system, as each pilot followed the one before him, creating a large formation behind the commander of the raid. A rare combination of technical perfection together with the best and most experienced pilots in the world, enabled them to achieve this very fine performance without any problem.

Each of the young pilots kept a fixed eye on the many instruments in front of him. The time was 16.00 and they turned north-east, crossing the border between Saudi Arabia and Iraq. They were concentrating on the small green radar screens in front of them, looking for any source of trouble or alarm. But none appeared to come. No enemy plane was trying to intercept them.

One more long and boring 30 minutes was behind them when they knew that almost half of the job was over. At 17.33 the leader and those who were close to him could identify the large buildings and the 60ft cement dome of the Tammuz project. The F-15s started climbing to a height of some thousand feet, in order to gain control over the combat area and make sure that no enemy planes were to disturb the Fighting Falcons in their mission. The F-16s were climbing only a few hundred feet. As pre-planned long months ago they were to bomb the Iraqi reactor from a low height, mainly to avoid the anti-aircraft fire of the Iraqis protecting the project.

No anti-aircraft gun had been fired yet, no SAM missile had been launched, when the first pilot dived his fighter bomber, aiming at the centre of the big cement dome under which the Tammuz I reactor was positioned. In less than five seconds he was climbing up again. The first two MK84 iron bombs had hit the concrete roof, exploding it into small pieces, when the second plane was already releasing its own ammunition. One by one, with intervals of no more than 10 seconds the Israeli Fighting Falcons bombed the reactor, while approaching it from different angles and directions. The Iraqi ZSU-23 anti-aircraft guns started firing at the attacking jets. The speed and precision of the raiders and their low-level flight left the Iraqi anti-aircraft defence no chance at all. The timing of the pilots, the accuracy of their bombs, were unbelievable. The long exercises of training in bombing a similar target in Israel now proved to be very efficient.

The last F-16 to drop the bombs was flown by Lieutenant Ilan Ramon. At the age of 27, and despite being the most junior pilot in the group, Ramon was one of the few pilots who knew the real mission target from start. He served as the navigation officer of the IAF's first F-16 squadron, and he took part in planning the optimal route to Osirak. As number 8 in the mission itself, he was in the most risky position: being the last one to bomb the reactor he was the pilot most exposed to the Iraqi anti-aircraft fire. But Ramon insisted on taking upon himself this position, maintaining that he was the only pilot with no children yet. When he broke to the left, after dropping his two MK84 bombs, he could clearly see that the target had already been seriously damaged. Starting to make his way back home, he had begun feeling, very much like his other colleagues, a certain sense of anti-climax. In his own words, a few days after the raid, 'You did a mission that was not much more complex than training missions.' More than 21 years later, Ramon would become the first Israeli astronaut and would lose his life in the tragic accident of space shuttle *Columbia* in early February 2003.

From the ground, some French technicians were watching the reactor's dome fly up in the air and explode into pieces. For one of them who was just on the way to his parked car it looked like a scene from a slow-motion movie. Fire caught quickly as the dome of the Osirak reactor collapsed and only a few metres of it now showed above the ground. The delicate parts of the reactor core, as well as its other components built under the ground, crashed into small metal pieces as each pair of bombs hit the centre of the target again and again.

For those on the ground the attack seemed to last hours. For the very busy Israeli pilots it seemed seconds. Altogether, within two minutes everything was over.

When the last bombing plane left the project area one of the F-15s left his colleagues who were covering from above. He was equipped with special photography devices, and took video pictures from above. Now he dived and took the last pictures of the ruined reactor. Smoke and fire covered the whole area but the pilot was able to take pictures of the scene with his special infra-red equipment.

After dropping their bombs, the F-16s were now much quicker than before. They were joined by the F-15s and altogether the 14-plane team started on the long way back to the air force bases in Israel.

In all, 16 MK84 iron bombs were dropped on the reactor. The accuracy of the bombing, considering the fact that no smart bombs were used, was astonishing. All but two were direct hits within 30 feet from the centre of the target. Later, the foreign press would claim that a secret Israeli agent had planted some electronic device in the reactor which enabled the bombs to home in on the centre of the project. This was false, but for many journalists the accuracy was so unbelievable that some fantastic and imaginative stories were necessary to explain it.

The planes were now flying in pairs at a very high altitude. They were well aware that this might lead to their interception, but they had no other choice. Flying just above ground level consumed much more fuel and now the jets were short of it. The pilots could only hope that no hostile fighters would intercept on their way back home, although they trusted their proven air-superiority in dogfights and were sure that if there was a skirmish they would prove it again.

No one, however, intercepted them, although certainly Jordanian, Iraqi and even Saudi radar stations detected the flying jets. It can be assumed that the planes were not intercepted due to lack of efficiency of the Arab airforces and some inferiority complex on the part of the Arab pilot compared to his Israeli adversary.

At 18.00 exactly the first F-16 landed back at Etzion. In the next ten minutes the rest of the planes landed in different air bases, scattered throughout Israel.

Eitan was now ready. He was connected to Begin's private house, where all the cabinet ministers were nervously waiting for the news. 'The mission is completed', reported the Israeli Chief of Staff to the worried Begin. 'All our planes returned safely to their bases.'

The Prime Minister was relieved. He informed his colleagues of the news. A bottle of Israeli brandy was brought and they all drank a toast of 'léhaim' to the Israeli Air Force.

High in the sky over Tel Aviv, two F-15s were 'buzzing off'

in a victory roll, after finishing the mission and before landing back at their base. They accelerated their speed, breaking the sound barrier. Two supersonic booms broke glasses in many homes. Nobody down below knew what had happened, but for the pilots it was a personal way of telling the worried Israeli citizens in the town that they no longer had to worry about the Iraqi reactor. The nightmare was over.

PART FOUR

JUDGMENT

'We have a great divergence in the administration. For now we are trying to speak right down the middle.'

(US State Department spokesman.)

'You can't help but admire their technical proficiency, although we strongly condemn the action.'

(US defence spokesman.)

'Privately, the White House was informed three hours after the attack. But President Reagan's strategists suspected that the Israelis hoped Washington would leak the news and thus give the impression of US collusion.'

(Jack Anderson, Washington Post, 23 June 1981.)

'The very survival of our civilization is placed at risk when the capacity to produce weapons of mass destruction is allowed to spread around the globe. We must all work together on this problem. There can be no more important task.'

(Open remarks of Senator Alan Cranston in his statement before the US Senate Foreign Relations Committee, Washington, DC, 18 June 1981.)

19

The Jerusalem Statement

'The Israeli Air Force yesterday attacked and destroyed the Osirak nuclear reactor which is near Baghdad. All our planes returned home safely.

The Government finds itself obligated to explain to enlighten public opinion why it decided on this special operation.

For a long time, we have followed with grave concern the construction of the Osirak nuclear reactor. Sources of unquestioned reliability told us that it was intended, despite statements to the contrary, for the production of atomic bombs.

The goal for these bombs was Israel. This was explicitly stated by the Iraqi ruler. After the Iranians slightly damaged the reactor, (Iraqi President) Saddam Hussein remarked that it was pointless for the Iranians to attack the reactor because it was being built against Israel alone.

The atomic bombs that this reactor would have been capable of producing, with enriched uranium or plutonium, were of the type dropped on Hiroshima. In this way, a danger to Israel's existence was being produced.

Highly reliable sources gave us two dates for the completion of the reactor and its operation: the first the beginning of July 1981, the second the beginning of September this year.

Within a short time, the Iraqi reactor would have been in operation and hot. In such conditions, no Israeli government could have decided to blow it up. This would have caused a huge wave of radioactivity over the city of Baghdad and its innocent citizens would have been harmed.

We were, therefore, forced to defend ourselves against the construction of an atomic bomb in Iraq which itself would not have hesitated to use it against Israel and its population centres.

Therefore, the Israeli Government decided to act without further delay to ensure the safety of our people.

The planning was precise. The operation was set for Sunday on an assumption that the 100 to 150 foreign experts who were active on the reactor would not be there on the Christian day of rest. This assumption proved correct. No foreign expert was hurt.

Two European governments were helping the Iraqi dictator in return for oil to manufacture nuclear weapons. Once again we call on them to desist from this terrible and inhuman act.

On no account shall we permit an enemy to develop weapons of mass destruction against the people of Israel.'

(Statement released by the Israeli government on the day following the raid.)

20

The Baghdad Statement

BAGHDAD: 8 JUNE 1981

'In the name of God, the merciful, the compassionate.

Great Iraqi people, sons of the glorious Arab nation, it has been known to us from the beginning that many parties, local and international, were and still are behind the eagerness of the backward and suspect Iranian regime to stir up the dispute with, conduct aggression against and begin the war against Iraq.

They have been behind the continuation of this war for several months because of their political and military support and backing for Iran, including information, technical consultations and direct and indirect military intelligence in order to achieve their evil objective against Iraq. The main party was the Zionist entity, which understands completely that a liberated, developed and capable Iraq is a decisive factor in determining the results of the Arab conflict against it, today and tomorrow.

The Zionist entity understands that one of the most decisive factors in determining the future of the conflict the Arab nation is waging against it is the continued presence of the technical and scientific gap between it and the Arab nation. Therefore, it is trying by all means to keep this gap within limits which will not enable the Arab nation to achieve victory over it in the conflict.

Based on this strategic objective, the Zionist enemy participated on more than one occasion directly and indirectly with Iran against Iraq. This included supplying Iran with military equipment and spare parts. Zionist enemy planes also raided Iraq in the first days of the war, thus exploiting the war circumstances against Iran, in collusion with the suspect regime in Iran. The raids were aimed in particular at the Iraqi nuclear installations.

We knew of and exposed the first attempt, which took place on 27 July 1980. At the time, we broadcast a statement about two raids on Baghdad. However, we did not mention the Zionist enemy by name for military and political reasons and for moral reasons and because we know from experience that declarations by Arab regimes about the participation of other parties in conflicts between them and the enemies were always coupled with failure as well as pretexts and justifications for this failure. That is why we hinted at the fact at the time and did not disclose all its details officially.

Compatriots, today we declare that the Zionist enemy planes yesterday carried out an air raid on Baghdad.

At 18.37 a formation of nine planes raided the nuclear installation. As on 27 September 1980, we preferred not to hasten in announcing this raid. As we were preparing this statement after completing all the evidence of this raid, the Zionist enemy this afternoon claimed responsibility for the raid. O brothers, sons of Iraq and sons of the Arab nation: this treacherous operation reveals to you a basic and important side of the reasons that prompted the suspect regime in Iran to kindle war with Iraq and continue this war for 10 months despite all the efforts that were exerted to avert it and to stop it on a just and honourable basis that would guarantee the legitimate rights and interests of both Iraq and Iran. The Zionist enemy is trying to achieve its objectives and to achieve for the rulers in Tehran and Qum what they have failed to achieve during the 10 months of this treacherous war.

They will not shake this giant revolution from its determination to be one with the masses and to express hopes and aspirations. The men who have been able through their loyalty to their people and nation, their faith in their cause and their minds and efforts, to bring Iraq's nuclear potential up to the standard which created this amount of rancour and blatant aggression by the Zionist and Persian enemies make us confident that they are also capable of continuing this trend no matter what our enemies can achieve in their attempts to do direct or indirect harm.

The road Iraq has taken in its victorious revolution – the road of freedom, independence and progress, the road of cohesion between the leadership and the masses – will not be abandoned. This road will remain wide open.

God willing, victory to our heroic people and glory to our Arab nation.'

(Statement released by the Revolutionary Command Council of Iraq on the day following the raid.)

21

Dropping Bombs and Clangers: Israel after the Raid

Monday, 8 June was the public holiday of Shavouth and thousands of Israelis spent the day on the beaches of Tel Aviv, Haifa and Eilat, swimming, sunbathing, talking or listening to their transistor radios.

At 3.30 in the afternoon, the Israeli Broadcasting Service dropped *its* bombshell on the Israeli people.

'We interrupt our regular broadcasting to announce a special statement.' The tension in the announcer's voice stopped all activity dead. 'The Israeli Air Force yesterday attacked and destroyed completely the Osirak nuclear reactor, which is near Baghdad. All our planes returned home safely.' The statement went on to explain the motives behind the attack. The shockwave reverberated throughout Israel. Friends telephoned each other, strangers stopped each other on the street. In less than an hour everyone knew what had happened. Soon radio and TV stations were relaying the news to the rest of the world.

But the true story behind the Israeli statement has still to be revealed.

While the raid was still in operation Begin asked his secretary to invite all his ministers and closest aides secretly to his apartment in Jerusalem. Each one received the invitation by phone and was not told why. The ministers were surprised to see each other and even more so when they found out why they had been invited. In this conspiratorial atmosphere they began to plot.

Immediately following the raid, Begin himself, together with his aides prepared an official statement. But because some of his ministers, as well as high-ranking officers in the army, especially in the intelligence and air-force sectors, preferred to avoid an official government admission that the raid had been carried out by the Israelis, it was agreed as a compromise that only after an Arab state had disclosed the fact of the raid would the Israelis release their official statement.

The Israeli intelligence officer-in-charge over the public holiday had received special instructions to report any special Arab news or other messages concerning Israeli activities in Iraq. The officer himself probably knew nothing of the raid. It was still considered top secret, even in Israel.

By noon one of the Israeli monitoring stations, which was listening to a public debate in the Jordanian parliament, monitored a speech given by the Jordanian Prime Minister, accusing Israeli planes of taking part in the Iran–Iran war, and of co-operating with the Iranians.

When this message was brought to the attention of the officer-in-charge, he quickly transmitted it to Begin's military aide. It is not exactly known what happened at this stage, but there are two possibilities: either the message was misunderstood and Begin's aides accepted it as an official Jordanian statement revealing the raid, or they used it as a means to publicize the statement which they had already prepared.

In any case, the time was close to 3.00 pm, and Begin's press officer called the Israeli radio station. He got through to the announcer in charge and dictated the official statement over the telephone. Since the press officer, Uri Porath, was new to the job and practically unknown to the radio staff, the announcer assumed this statement to be a bad joke. He did not believe him and at 3.00 the statement was not read out during the regular news broadcast. But an employee at the radio station, who happened to be related to Begin, called the Prime Minister.

'Uncle', he said, 'we've just got this ridiculous statement from someone who claims to be your press officer. We did not broadcast it because we thought it unbelievable.'

Begin was very angry. He had wanted the statement transmitted as soon as possible and now there was this stupid and unnecessary delay. He gave his nephew instructions to stop all programmes and release the statement. So at 3.30 Kol Yisrael

(The Voice of Israel) interrupted its programmes to broadcast the dramatic message.

One of the reasons why – if not the most important of them all – Begin and his aides were anxious to release the statement concerning the raid was the internal political revenue which they expected as a fringe benefit of the successful operation. The Israeli elections were to be held in another three weeks and Begin badly needed the votes. For the past year and a half the Israeli as well as foreign media had considered his administration to be a failure. Now, he had to prove that he was the right man to lead Israel in this troubled and dangerous period.

Although, following the raid, both Begin and his colleagues in the Likud Party claimed that they would not use the IAF operation as a weapon in their election campaign, almost everybody in Israel was aware of the timing of the raid – it was now very close to election day.

Begin himself made a series of extraordinarily stupid blunders following the raid. Some of them can be put down to negligence in preparing to explain the necessity of the attack to the public. The Israeli Foreign Office of course did not know about the impending raid and therefore could not possibly prepare a campaign to explain the need for it. Thus Begin quoted Saddam Hussein as saying on 4 October 1980 that the Iraqi reactor was aimed against Israel.

It was a useful quotation, but it was revealed a week later that Hussein had never said anything like that on this particular date. The Israeli Foreign Office then had to instruct all its press attachés throughout the world to stop using the quote. For Yehuda Bloom, the Israeli Ambassador to the UN, who had mainly based his speech in the UN assembly on this quotation, the message to stop using it arrived just in time. Now the perturbed Bloom had to look for a new one. Fortunately there were many speeches by Hussein in which he had hinted that the aim of the Iraqi nuclear reactor was Israel's destruction. Mr Bloom did not have to work too hard:

> In connection with the Zionist entity's campaign against the Iraqi use of nuclear technology: the rich and glorious past of Iraq will only be appreciated when it spills its wrath on the Zionist entity and when such technology is

harnessed to the cause of the Arab nations. Iraq will use it for the freeing of Palestine and for no other purpose.

(Statement by Saddam Hussein, 19 August 1980, as reported by the Iraqi State News Agency.)

In connection with the Iraqi–Saudi [joint statement] to boycott states which transfer their embassies to Jerusalem, the best decision actually is to destroy Tel-Aviv with bombs. However what we must [now] do is to use all the weapons at our disposal until we can answer the foe with bombs. Only our Arab brethren could bring about co-operation in this area.

(Statement by Saddam Hussein, same date, as reported by Radio Baghdad.)

A few days later Begin made an even more serious mistake. At a party in the house of the new British Ambassador to Israel, Patrick Moberly, he said that the Israeli planes had destroyed a secret underground laboratory in the reactor site. He even gave the exact depth of the laboratory: 40 metres (120ft) beneath earth level.

Everybody was shocked. If Israeli planes could destroy a hidden target 40 metres below the reactor, Israel had an astonishing air-strike capability. It also meant that the Iraqis did have some secret installation which neither the French scientists nor the IAEA knew anything about. It was a very good argument for the attack, and reporters and news editors raced to get the story out.

But 24 hours later it was revealed that the Israeli premier had made a mistake. From his office came an apology. The PM had meant only 4 metres (12 feet) and not 40. The Quai d'Orsay described Begin's latest declaration concerning the secret lab as 'pure imagination', and American sources admitted that they did not know what Begin was talking about. Israeli Air Force Chief in Command David Ivri, when asked on Israeli television what he had to say about Begin's 'secret-lab' story, replied stonily that he had nothing to say about it. But it was clear that the 'story' was very serious after the propaganda fiasco following the raid.

But the biggest rebuff Begin had to suffer after the raid did not come from outside Israel but from a very close group of men whom Begin had cause to appreciate: the pilots who had carried out the raid to perfection.

A large proportion of Israeli pilots came from Kibbuzim and Moshavim. These sectors tend to vote for the Labour Party and had been strongly against Begin and his performance as Israeli PM.

Begin decided that he would like a close talk with the pilots who had executed the raid – and to have himself photographed with them. It meant a lot to him personally and for his election campaign. It was agreed therefore that the pilots would be invited to a special government meeting a week after the raid.

But the pilots refused to come.

Some of them had made it clear to close friends that they had carried out the mission for the existence of the people of Israel, and not for the existence of Begin as Prime Minister. So the Israeli government decided that if the Mountain would not come to Menachem then Menachem would have to go to the Mountain. Begin and his ministers made up their minds to visit the air base from which the pilots had taken off and meet them personally there.

This time the pilots did not have any choice. They had to meet Begin, but they still had one ace up their sleeve. When Begin and his colleagues came to the headquarters of the air base where the pilots were waiting for them, they found a nice line of parked cars in front of the building – the private cars of the pilots. On the back and the front windows of each car big stickers were displayed calling for the support of Shimon Peres, the opposition leader, and against Menachem Begin's party, Likud.

The Israeli premier and some of his colleagues blushed. They fully understood the pilots' meaning. As one of Israel's top columnists later wrote, for years the Labour Party had been trying to beat Begin. Now, some pilots, most of whom came from the left-wing sector and were against Begin, had flown for some hours, risking their lives for their country, and had completed the mission successfully, only to find that they had lent massive support to Begin's electoral chances.

The fact that the elections were so close to the time of the raid and the fact that each political party was trying to gain political capital from the raid could have been very harmful to Israel's security. When government ministers were not attempting to prove that they had always been for, and not against, the raid, the opposition leaders were claiming that Begin had been informed by Israeli intelligence services that the Iraqi nuclear reactor was not going to be operational in July (as Begin had claimed to excuse the raid) and would be unlikely to go 'hot' before September. Thus, they argued, the decision to strike in June had been a mere election tactic by an opportunist prime minister clutching at a potent political straw.

It is little wonder that in this highly charged atmosphere – the 1981 elections in Israel were probably more hysteria-ridden than any previous elections in Israel's history – secret details about the raid started to be leaked. Among them was Begin's claim that there had been co-operation with the USA concerning the Iraqi research.

The impression the Israeli public received during these three tense weeks between the raid and the election day was that their prime minister was revealing one secret after another in order to win the elections.

It was not only the impression of the general public, but also of the head of Mossad, even the name of whom was considered then to be a state secret (although it had already been published in *Time*, *Newsweek* and other US magazines as General (res.) Yitzhak Hoffi). He took an unprecedented step: he gave an interview to the Israeli daily *Ha Aretz*, in which he demanded that all talk about the raid should cease immediately. He claimed that all these leaks had already harmed Israel's security. Some foreign intelligence services which had unofficially co-operated with Israel's intelligence in the past, would have second thoughts after all the debate in Israel concerning the raid.

This unprecedented interview with the head of Mossad was only made possible because he gave it without first consulting Begin. He knew that Begin would have refused because the main source of the leaks was Begin himself.

When the Prime Minister summoned him to his office and admonished him, he apologized but the fact remained: he had made his point. All talk concerning the raid was to be stopped immediately.

While the raid was brilliantly planned and executed, the aftermath in Israel was amateurish in the extreme, mainly because of the election debacle, but also because of Begin's behaviour. Israel had performed a great service to the whole world by destroying the Iraqi reactor, which had been against the interests of every peace-loving country, but still, because of Begin's indiscretion and the failure of a counter-propaganda campaign, Israel was blamed as a pirate state that had flouted international law. It was outlawed by the IAEA and condemned in the UN assembly.

Having succeeded in carrying out a professional raid over one of the most threatening projects to its existence, Israel failed in explaining why it had needed to do it. Perhaps typically for those who are good at the military side of things, in deeds and not in words, the Israelis had completely neglected to prepare and to launch a follow-up public relations campaign to explain the raid to world public opinion.

22

The Propaganda War: Hussein Hits Backs

The raid on the Tammuz project surprised the whole world. It surprised the Americans as well as the Russians, Europe as well as China, and even the Israelis themselves. But most of all it shocked the Arab world and especially the Iraqi regime.

Although for more than two years the Iraqis were well aware that a secret war was being fought against their most ambitious project, and even after the Iranian air attack in September 1980, the Iraqi defence system as well as the political leadership were still shocked by the Israeli raid.

There are not many details about what happened in Baghdad during the first 24 hours following the raid. One thing was clear to everybody who carefully analyzed the Iraqi reaction in this 24 hours: the Iraqis had no idea who had carried out the bombardment, nor exactly what was damaged, nor how the raid was carried out. All control systems in Baghdad seem to have been in total chaos. The Iraqi president, the strong man of the Ba'athist regime, had suddenly disappeared. Aides, who were looking for him to inform him of the raid and to receive his instructions, could not trace him for six hours or so.

At a press conference in Rome the Iraqi Ambassador to Italy, Taha Ahmed el Dahud, caused a sensation when he admitted five days later that until the Israeli statement came out his government had had no idea who had carried out the raid.

Under these circumstances it was quite clear that the official Israeli announcement concerning the surprise attack came as the second shock for Saddam Hussein's regime.

Now the Iraqi revolutionary regime had no other choice but to admit that its most ambitious project, Tammuz 17, had been hit by an Israeli air raid. On the evening of 8 June the Revolutionary Command of Iraq issued a statement in which, for the first time, it reacted to the Israeli raid.

The beginning of the statement mainly described the so-called 'Israeli political and military support and backing for Iran'. It then went on to blame Israel for trying to destroy every Arabic effort to close the scientific gap between the Arab world and the 'Zionist entity'. Israel was again accused of involvement in the war between Iraq and Iran, probably to explain Iraq's lack of success in the war. On this basis the statement went on: 'Compatriots, today we declare that the Zionist enemy planes yesterday carried out an air raid on Baghdad. At 18.37[1] a formation of nine planes raided the nuclear installation.'

To explain the fact that, in spite of the chaos in Baghdad immediately after the raid, the Iraqi regime had waited more than 24 hours before admitting it, the statement continued: 'As on 27 September 1980, we preferred not to hasten in announcing this raid. As we were preparing this statement after completing all the evidence of this raid, the Zionist enemy this afternoon claimed responsibility for the raid.'

The statement then tried to attach some special meaning to the Israeli surprise in connection with the Iraqi–Iranian war: 'The Zionist enemy is trying to achieve its objectives and to achieve for the rulers in Tehran and Qum what they have failed to achieve during the 10 months of this treacherous war.'

The Iraqi statement ended with a promise to the people of Iraq that the road the Ba'athist leadership has taken so far would go on to lead the people to freedom, independence and progress.

A day later, Iraqi government spokesmen had become even more rigid in their attitude towards Israel:

The Zionist attacks on the Iraqi nuclear installation twice[2] within a period of several months clearly emphasize the fact that the Zionist enemy knows that Iraq, with its sophisticated and technological war potential, will be at the forefront of the Arab forces destined to clash with the Zionist enemy in any future nationalist campaign. Iraq, with its sophisticated military potential, will be in the front lines of any further national confrontation with the Zionist enemy.

Radio Baghdad went on broadcasting this type of propaganda for hours. In the Arab world the written or broadcast word is sometimes even more persuasive and meaningful than personal experience. The regime in Baghdad had been severely humiliated and its prestige was at stake. Saddam Hussein knew that he could not react against Israel by force – at least not immediately. The media propaganda campaign against Israel was the most he could do to release the frustration of the leadership, as well as the people of Iraq, after the raid which had showed how exposed they were to an Israeli strike. But it was still interesting to note that Saddam Hussein himself kept quiet for ten days after the raid. As the leader of the Iraqi people, he probably knew that some other reaction apart from the propaganda campaign against Israel was needed.

NOTES

1. Iraqi time.
2. The Iraqis refer to the Iranian air raid of September 1980 as a raid carried out by Israel and not by Iran.

144

23

A Delicate Balancing Act: The American Reaction

Following the destruction of the Iraqi reactor the Middle East would never be the same. The balance of power in the Middle East and the Gulf had been changed inexorably.

The nuclear revolution had finally penetrated this precarious, unstable but strategically vital region and the annihilation of the Iraqi reactor tore apart the rules of international behaviour previously known in the Middle East. The Israeli action was the first destruction of an enemy's nuclear reactor, preventing by force the proliferation of nuclear weapons and establishing a serious international precedent.

With the destruction of the reactor, Israel and PM Begin created for themselves a nuclear monopoly in the Middle East. The international community can debate endlessly whether Israel really destroyed Iraq's nuclear capacity, but what has happened is in the long run more far-reaching than Mr Begin could ever have intended. The Arab world received a shock of 1967 proportions, a shock which reparations or censures in the UN would not lessen. The Arabs sought revenge after 1967 and they would do so again, to the extent that nuclear proliferation was expected to speed up in Libya, Syria, Egypt, Pakistan and certainly again in Iraq. What Israel has succeeded in doing was to buy itself some time – a commodity that always runs out.

The insider, the military analyst of the respectable *Ha'Aretz*, Zeev Schiff, clearly stated: 'Following the destruction of the Iraqi reactor PM Begin established and proclaimed a new and unbending rule in Israel's security policy ... Israel will not permit the Arabs to equip themselves with instruments of mass annihilation' (19 July 1981). This monopoly doctrine, not unlike that of the US during 1945–50, clearly stated that neither this government nor hopefully another (i.e. a moderate Labour government) would henceforth tolerate such instruments, especially when these states are governed by such irrational and rejectionist leaders as Saddam Hussein and Gaddafi whose sole purpose in dealing with Israel is its annihilation. Begin did not state his views on whether, if moderate Arab states possessed such weapons, Israel should also regard their destruction as imperative. One can only assume that such a distinction *is* made, as is the case with Egypt, which renounced war as an instrument of policy towards Israel.

In fact one could speculate as to why moderate Arab regimes seek weapons of total annihilation if this is not an element of national policy as it is with Saddam Hussein and Muamar Gaddafi. It also became imperative, for the sake of Israeli deterrence policy to destroy the reactor in a period when the conventional military ratio between Israel and the Arab states had turned against Israel: in the early 1980s it seemed that 'Israel cannot sustain its conventional military superiority for long, and by 1985 the Arabs will have a five-to-one superiority in numbers and in military equipment'.

This goes back to the Ben Gurion–Dayan–Peres flexible-response concept of deterrence: Israel's IDF and conventional weapons are not sufficient to deter Arab states, as the wars of 1967, 1973 and the 1968–70 war of attrition demonstrated. Behind the Arabs there also then lurked the Soviet threat while American power does not guarantee Israel's post-1967 borders at all.

Begin and his advisers were hoping that western Europe, especially France and Italy, would now be deterred from providing Iraq with lethal fissionable material. After October 1980 and probably before, the US intelligence community perceived that Israel was up to something; Israel certainly did not hide the fact. It had urged the Carter administration to impose strong diplomatic pressure upon the French and Italians against their delivering nuclear equipment and material to Iraq. This of course was to no avail. The arrogant Giscardian regime paid no heed to Israeli or American requests and warnings.

Thus after October 1980 the US was aware of the purposes and principles that motivated this decision, even if they knew nothing of the secret cabinet meeting. What the US did not know and what it was not consulted about (and thus Secretary Casper Weinberger's reflex action in embargoing the delivery of four F-16s to Israel scheduled to arrive a few days after the raid) was the *timing* and the *system* planned by Israel, and the process of training simulation and air force preparedness for the attack. Washington was not consulted on the decision to destroy the Iraqi reactor.

For the American intelligence community, the timing of the bombing was a total surprise – even if it was aware of Israel's serious apprehensions regarding the nature and purpose of the reactor.

The American reaction was one of surprise, dismay and concern. Seemingly, Israel had wiped out General Haig's concept of strategic consensus and American policy in the area. Also, despite the Reagan administration's relative indifference to the general problem of nuclear proliferation, the reaction to the Israeli raid was confused, swift and unpleasant.

Amid the furore over the sale of AWACS to Saudi Arabia following the Weinberger Joint Chief's decision to go ahead with the deal, one thing had become increasingly clear: the United States – the Reagan administration – had no clear overall policy in the Middle East and the Persian Gulf. Rather, it was subsisting on leftover strands of old, worn, Nixon and Carter initiatives.

Secretary Haig and the administration decided to 'postpone' a decision on Middle East-Persian Gulf strategy for at least the first six months of the administration. The Middle East, however, does not stand still, and Palestinians, Egyptians, Iraqis and Syrians make political and military decisions which nevertheless involve the great powers. Secretary Haig – following the grand designs of the President that East–West relations would, in American strategy, dominate over the North–South Carterite conception, and that the US must confront Soviet military imperialism and international terrorism represented by the PLO head-on – was inventing a new doctrine for the Middle East strategic consensus, whereby Israel and the Arabs would presumably be brought together in a collective security arrangement under American protection, with international communism and terrorism as the common foe.

The concept of strategic consensus was a non-starter. It was the other side of the Carter–Brzezinsky comprehensive settlement policy. The policy of comprehensive settlement aspired to bring Israel and the Arab states into an overall peace conference. This was utopian. The policy of strategic consensus, however, aspired to bring Israel and the Arabs into a common war council designed to protect the Middle East from the Soviets. This aspiration was no less chimeric.

Strategic consensus was a recent American invention to deal with the Middle East problem. The idea and the hope was that Arab moderates such as Egypt, Jordan, Saudi Arabia (and hopefully Syria and Iraq) and Israel would be supplied with the necessary weapons to meet the Soviet challenge. Thus each country on a bilateral and eventually on a collective basis – a kind of Middle Eastern NATO – would be protected by an American anti-Soviet umbrella. This strategic idea was unrealistic as long as the so-called Arab moderates, Saudi Arabia and Jordan, supported and in fact were allied with the Arab rejectionists like Iraq and the PLO.

As long as the Arab rejectionist front was financed by the sheikhs of the Arabian peninsula and the Iraqi Army was Soviet-equipped, there was little chance for a common Arab–Israeli anti-Soviet front. In fact strategic consensus came as a substitute for strategic balance, the American formula for the Middle East in the previous four decades. Previously, strategic considerations were based on an Arab–Israel military ratio of 1:3 and both the US and Israel sought to maintain this balance. This was based at that time on the nations' capability, not their aspirations.

The new concept could in fact have upset the military balance in the Middle East in favour of the Arab states. Under the strategic consensus doctrine the US need not refrain from practically arming without limits the Middle East and the Gulf, only subject to these countries' wealth.

Strategic consensus could have become a military arsenal that even the US, however much in command and in control, might one day have found to be a revolutionary inferno led either by a Saudi Gaddafi or, worse, a Saudi Sunni Khomeini. Saudi Arabia is a weak state. At the time, some CIA analysts doubted whether the dynasty would last until the end of the

1980s. Why, then 'Iranianize' Saudi Arabia, which in any case could never have integrated its acquired weapons? The Israelis who were excited about strategic consensus erred as much as their American counter-parts. The Arabs considered Israel not the USSR their primary foe. The best statement of the American position was that of former US Secretary of Defense, James Schlesinger:

> The administration's approach in the Mideast has been to focus on the Soviet threat and to seek a 'strategic consensus' presumably ending in cooperative action of the states of the region in improving the military deterrent to Soviet intervention. While such an outcome would be highly satisfying to many of us, it is the height of American ethnocentrism to assume that the states of the region will abandon their immediate concerns and embrace our own. For both Israel and its Arab neighbors, worry about the other's intentions and actions constitutes a clear and present danger, which they will scarcely forget simply to accommodate our concern regarding the longer term though lower-probability threat to the region posed by the Soviet Union. Any hope that regional attention could be focused northward, in the absence of a simultaneous and effective grappling with the internal tensions of the region, must now be abandoned. The raid, in short, means the end for that particular drift in American policy preferences, for it has sharpened the apprehensions about the unresolved internal conflicts, while raising increased doubts about the effectiveness of the American role in the region.
>
> With regard to these regional tensions, the United States might have preferred to temporize. It can do so no longer. The raid makes these tensions central – and underscores US inability to fulfil its expected role of ensuring Israeli restraint. The United States will now be forced to choose. On the one hand, we may tacitly condone the raid by maintaining arms shipments to Israel. The inevitable consequence will be a further breach between the United States and much of the Arab world. On the other hand, a cessation of arms shipments will automatically bring into

question the depth of the American commitment to
Israel's security. Forcing this choice on the United States
was hardly in Israel's interests.

To condone the attack – including Israel's use of
American supplied weapons in a manner dubious under
American law – requires in logic a far higher priority for
anti-proliferation policies than the administration has
exhibited to date. Senator Alan Cranston and others may
quite consistently, in view of their long-term stress on preventing the spread of nuclear weapons, find the Israeli strike
justifiable. So could the Carter administration, with its well-
advertised, if ineffective, policies to prevent proliferation.
But, to date, the Reagan administration has been indifferent
or fatalistic about the spread of nuclear weapons, perhaps
most dramatically so in terms of its evolving support and
military assistance for Pakistan. Having immediately condemned the attack, the administration will find it doubly
hard subsequently to condone it on the basis of non-
proliferation objectives to which it so far has been rather
indifferent. If the arms flow to Israel continues, in the face
of the proprieties of American law, the distrust of American
motives and of its intended role as honest broker in revolv-
ing Arabi–Israeli differences will be significantly height-
ened.

Since Israel's own power is quite limited, its unilateral
effort to prevent the spread of nuclear weapons in the
region will prove, at best, transient. An issue on which the
superpowers agree, though even they are limited in their
ability to grapple with the problems, is certainly beyond
Israel's very limited abilities. Israel's action may, by dram-
atizing the issue, strengthen Arab determination to acquire
nuclear weapons. Perhaps more significant, it should be
recalled that the initial move toward 'the Islamic bomb'
and the soliciting of support for that venture was by
Pakistan's Ali Bhutto in the middle 1970s. And, despite
Begin's provocative rhetoric, Pakistan lies beyond the
reach of Israeli war planes and is, moreover, under
American protection.

To prevent the spread of nuclear weapons in the region,
Israel's own power is far too limited. The best that might be

hoped for from Israel's badly-thought-through though brilliantly executed strike is that it could once again focus international attention on the problem of proliferation. Yet, it will do so in a badly deteriorated international climate.

(J. R. Schlesinger, *Washington Post*, 12 June 1981.)

It was a folly to proclaim that Israel was a bastion against the USSR. The 1973 War did not prove that. In fact it was America and not Israel who came to the aid of the so-called Israeli anti-communist 'defender'. Strategic consensus was not a policy but a catastrophe. There were other ways to establish an Israeli–Saudi rapprochement. The only structure upon which a Middle Eastern policy could be erected was the Camp David process, and it was within this process that an American–Israeli–Arab strategy eventually could mature.

The US from the 1960s had been notoriously zealous about the spread of nuclear weapons. First there was France's *Force de Frappé*, then smaller Third World nations joined in the process of becoming nuclear – India, Pakistan, Taiwan, South Africa, Iraq, Israel, Libya and possibly others. The US finally established an international legal instrument, the Non-Proliferation Treaty (NPT), to which most of the Third World and other smaller nations are signatories. Israel and India are notorious exceptions.

Yet the NPT is not a powerful enough instrument to prevent nuclear proliferation. After all, Iraq is an NPT signatory yet it has nevertheless been in the process of creating a nuclear capability. The NPT has become a liberal American ideology as well as a mechanism to ensure that the international nuclear club does not spread. The IAEA, a UN agency established to monitor nuclear proliferation, and not unlike the UN itself, is highly politicised. For instance, in the Iraqi case, only representatives of what Iraq perceived to be friendly nations inspected Iraq's reactor – and rather superficially at that.

The IAEA hypocrisy is quite clear: why did it not withdraw India's credentials, although it was expected to take away Israel's, when India is as much a nuclear state as Israel in the eyes of the international community, especially the US? The US after 1960 made continual visits to Dimona but these were stopped in the mid-1960s. Carter's administration especially was unhappy about Israel's failure to comply with the NPT. The pressure on Israel in that area was changed according to the orientation of succeeding American administrations. The US was certainly concerned about the Iraqi reactor, the Carter administration for instance, put pressure on France so that the French would not use enriched uranium supplied by the US to French laboratories.

Thus the surprised and angry American reaction, although not unexpected in Israel, was still disturbing. Especially when it was felt that the US had failed to understand what disturbed Israel; that nuclear weapons in the hands of fanatic dictators and unscrupulous terrorists committed to the annihilation of Israel was a *casus belli* for it and that there was no way Israel – and for that matter any government of Israel – would allow itself to be at the mercy of ultimate weapons owned by the most degenerate regime in the Middle East.

The American reaction on the public-opinion level was even more inexplicable to Israel. Why would the American media, the chief editorials of the most influential US papers come out so strongly against Israel? Was it a case of misconception: that Israel was Goliath, the Arabs' David? *Or* is it that the 'Christian' world once more was oblivious to Jewish dangers and survival? Yet all this happened. The media in the first days after the attacks went out of its way to condemn the Israeli action (the *Wall Street Journal* excluded) and voices in Congress, including Israel's friends, were raised in an indiscriminate chorus against it.

The knee-jerk reaction of *The New York Times* and *Washington Post*, calling Israel's attack 'sneaky', 'an act of inexcusable and short-sighted aggression' (9 June), says more about the editorialists of *The New York Times* than about Israel or the US. The *Washington Post* went even further: 'In knocking out the Iraqi nuclear reactor the Israelis have made a grievous error. They did not act lightly, but they acted, we believe, in a way contrary to their own long-term interests and in a way contrary to American interests as well' (9 June). In fact, of course, the US government was well aware of the Iraqi threat and in fact the Israeli raid had contributed to American interests.

After the raid Begin sent an explanatory note to Reagan in

which he said that, had the Iraqis dropped a nuclear bomb on
the Tel Aviv area, it was expected that 60,000 Israelis would
have been casualties. This fact was not published in Israel in
order to avoid panic. General Sharon (in an interview) estimated that a similar attack would cause 50,000 deaths and 150,000
radiation casualties. Though President Reagan was sympathetic
to Israel's anxiety and concern, he faced a certain dilemma in
his initial response to the raid: he recognized a need to distance
the US from the raid and not to be indulgent towards Israel, but
he also saw good reason not to call the basic American attitude
towards Israel into question. He condemned the raid but did
nothing to alter the US's continuing role as Israel's sole patron
and sole foreign source of arms. President Reagan reassured the
Israeli Ambassador in Washington that the attack would not
affect US–Israeli relations. 'The President reaffirmed our strong
and deeply-rooted relationship with Israel and said a *qualitative
imbalance* would not be allowed to grow in the area.'

In seeking ways to punish Israel for the raid on Iraq there
was a great divergence in the administration: another reason
why when the President empathized with the victim of aggressive Israel his bureaucrats became confused. As respectable
columnist George Will wrote: 'Without endorsing that assessment of its [Iraq's] nuclear capability Israel can reply that deterrence assumes a degree of rationality that cannot be assumed
regarding the volatile leadership classes of many nations, and
least of all Iraq, which has a reputation for ferocity and insta-
bility notable even in their region. Israeli leaders, who know
that one nuclear weapon used against Tel Aviv would destroy
Israel, cannot responsibly rest Israel's security on the soothing
assertion that its enemies are technologically backward but
politically sophisticated' (*Washington Post*, 14 June).

The *Los Angeles Times'* editorial, asking if Israel's case was
credible, concluded: 'Israel is and will continue to take a lot of
international heat for what has happened. The irony is that
Israel, by its discomfiting action, may in the end have made the
Middle East a somewhat safer place for all concerned' (11
June).

The *Wall Street Journal* summarized the US schizophrenia
clearly:

From the time the raid occurred, the US behaved as if it were possible to walk right down the middle of this issue and get out with skin on both sides of the body unburned. On the one hand President Reagan expressed sympathy with the Israeli dilemma. But there was a lot going on, on the other hand, designed to appeal to Arab opinion ... In short, the process is turning out to be yet another lesson in how we can manage to fray our relationship with Israel, buy ourselves no respect from Israel's Arab adversaries, weaken our position as a trustworthy go-between in a Mideast peace process, and more generally tarnish our reputation for leadership in the world.

It is a loser's game: There is no way we can punish Israel enough to satisfy its enemies without taking alarming bites out of Israel while demonstrating to other Mideast nations what we can do for them at the same time is a vastly more promising strategy. The Carter administration, by both its failures and its successes, demonstrated this; we thought the Reagan people had come into office knowing it. Fortunately, there's still a little time to learn. (7 July)

The Israeli attack had sparked off a harsh and instant reaction in the US, where it was formally condemned on 8 June 1981 as 'unprecedented'. US-supplied uranium weapons used in the raid, the US authorities said, may have violated American law. In the strongest language used by any US administration in years to protest an action of Israel's the State Department had already prepared a report on 'possible violation' of the law regarding arms exports, demanding that it be submitted to Congress 'very swiftly'.

The administration's reaction came after a number of Arab ambassadors in Washington had privately called on the US to dissociate itself from the attack. The fact still remained that the US, caught by surprise, had reacted belatedly.

The US was hence struggling to find a way to chastise Israel – without significantly cutting military aid – for using American-made planes in its air strike against Iraq. White House, State Department and Pentagon officials were heatedly debating what to do.

'We have a great divergence in the administration', one State Department official said. 'For now we are trying to speak right down the middle.'

While President Reagan was mulling over the problem, Secretary Weinberger was taking a clear line. He put it in terms of how substantial the violation might have been. 'If the violation is found to be substantial Israel will be ineligible for future arms transfers from the US.'

On 9 June, Secretary Haig told Congress that Israel might have committed 'a substantial violation' of its arms agreement with the US by using American-built planes for the bombing of the reactor. Under the Arms Export Control Act, the President has the authority to suspend aid if it so determined. Instead, Secretary Haig said that while the administration continued talks with Israel and while Congress held hearings on the matter, 'the President had directed the suspension *for the time being* of the immediate shipment of four F-16 aircraft which had been scheduled this week'.

Congressional leadership response to the President was positive. Clement Zablocki, Chairman House Foreign Affairs Committee, criticized the bombing and said the President's decision was 'a measure and prudent one. It is also necessary.' Senator Charles Percy, Chairman Senate Foreign Relations Committee and no friend of Israel, was harsher in his comments. He charged that the raid 'may undercut' the diplomatic efforts (Saudi launched) of Ambassador Philip Habib, and made 'even dimmer the possibility of building toward middle peace on the Camp David model'. This kind of statement could easily have been issued in Riad or Amman.

Senator Alfone D'Amato, a New York-Italian Conservative Republican, differed. 'The bombing was perfectly proper legitimate and it was a pre-emptive strike that should have been expected', he said. Senator Daniel Moynihan, senior Democrat from New York, agreed. 'The Israelis did what they had to do. Anything that takes out a nuclear installation I am in favour of.' Senator Alan Cranston, one of the most respectable Democratic leaders in the Senate and a member of the Senate's Foreign Relations Committee, deeply regretted the decision to delay the F-16 deliveries.

Thus facing a quandary, the Reagan administration actually

issued a limited rebuke, a 'very measured response', balancing Israel's anxiety about a potential nuclear threat with its own credibility in the Middle east, while controlling its own sales policies. But the F-16 suspension was less harsh than the Ford–Kissinger Reassessment Policy in August 1975, when the whole US–Israel military relationship was reassessed after Prime Minister Rabin had temporarily suspended negotiations over the Sinai II shuttle disengagement diplomacy.

Privately, administration officials made plain that this was more a political than legal question, one the administration needed to consult with Congress. Members of Congress said that House majority leaders felt 'an instinctive, an inherent sympathy for Israel's plight'.

Though Secretary Weinberger sought to punish Israel strongly, clearly Washington did not condone such an act. Despite no opposition to the suspension of the F-16s, National Security officials privately applauded the boldness and efficiency of the Israeli air strike on an ally of the Soviet Union.

Prime Minister Begin personally attacked Secretary Weinberger for his attitude. In fact he denounced both Mr Weinberger and Shimon Peres for 'deliberate false propaganda' on his and Israel's real motivations for the raid. He charged Weinberger with trying to persuade Reason to curtail Israeli military and economic aid. Weinberger responded by calling the charge 'erroneous'.

It has been argued by many, both in Israel and other countries, that the biggest mistake committed by the Begin government was not the decision to launch the raid but to admit it. By leaving the identity of the raid ambiguous Israel could have avoided the inevitable outcry that followed. It would have avoided embarrassing the US government, which was trying to improve its relationship with the Arab world.

On 11 June Reagan met with Arab and Israeli officials to calm the Middle East crisis. The President, however, went out of his way to reassure Israelis of 'no fundamental re-evaluations of relationships' and 'reaffirmed our strong and deeply-rooted relationship with Israel'. Despite Arab ambassadors' demands for harsher measures against Israel, the President did not budge.

By 22 June, Israelis were predicting the early resumption of American shipments of F-16s. This would combine the four F-16s delayed on 10 June with the next batch that had been ordered. All, however, was changed when on 23 June Israel bombed PLO headquarters in Beirut. The F-16 order was suspended and the embargo was not lifted until 17 August. Only on 1 September were the first four F-16s released.

Ironically, on 11 August, when Israel's Foreign Office issued a communiqué describing the US action as 'unjust and damaging' and a 'breach of contract', President Sadat visited Washington to sign a US–Egyptian arms deal (to include tanks and missiles). It was necessary, said the US administration, to 'maintain a balance' in the Middle East.

24

Israel's Verdict

In October 1980 the decision to destroy the nuclear reactor after a stormy but not critical debate had been taken by a majority in the Israeli cabinet after a minority had pushed for the action. The debate, which was confined to experts and lower-echelon security bureaucrats, has never been made public – only glimpses of it have appeared in the press. What's more the debate was over timing, which was inextricably linked to the development of the Tammuz project, which had been monitored as closely as possible. All members of the cabinet's ministerial committee for security, including traditional doves Yigael Yadin, Yoseph Burg and Simcha Ehrhich, were in favour of working against Iraq's nuclear armament. Once again there was no consensus in this group over timing or the method of destruction.

Opposition to the plan was not so much against the destruction of the reactor – rather, they feared the political fall-out that could be expected, whether it succeeded or not, a possible crisis in Israeli–American relations; the weakening of Sadat's influence in the Arab world; the enhancing of dormant Arab dreams of unity; the Iraqi reaction, which might well be to continue and once again accelerate its nuclear potential; and, above all, the disastrous effects should the operation fail.

The immediate debate of October 1980 needs to be viewed in the context of a wrangle which had been going on for over a decade. The debate over nuclear policy had originally developed when Israel's reactor went 'hot', somewhere around 1968, and two schools of thought had emerged. The strategic hawks sought nuclear monopoly and superiority (it is this school of thought that has obviously triumphed). They articulated a theory of flexible response. They believed that an Israeli nuclear monopoly and superiority would eventually lead to a solution of the Arab–Israeli conflict on Israel's terms.

The doves, who are usually associated with the Labour Party or the left, saw no reason to delay proliferation – the development of nuclear capacities among the other Middle East nations. They argued that Israel could not sustain its conventional military superiority for long, that by 1985 the Arabs would have a five-to-one superiority in numbers and in military equipment. A nuclear stability or nuclear stand-off, they argued, would create peace and stability. They saw a future in which borders and territories would become unimportant: Israeli technological superiority would be sufficient for survival against the Arabs.

In justifying the reactor attack, Begin reasoned that Israel was the rational state in the Middle East and could not allow an irrational state such as Iraq to have a nuclear capability. The hawkish position here was that deterrence would never be a practical weapon. The asymmetry in the nuclear equilibrium in the Middle East could work only for the rational side. The hawks, in short, preferred the static situation of an Israeli nuclear monopoly as opposed to the fluid position of the doves.

Begin's opponent in the upcoming election, Labour leader Shimon Peres, had been highly critical of the attack. He had charged that, in spite of the fact that Iraqi President Saddam Hussein was indeed irresponsible, it was not necessary to bomb the reactor, that in fact Israel could have waited five years to do so. Peres argued that international pressure, meaning his close connections to France's Socialist President, François Mitterrand, could have somehow obliterated the Iraqi reactor diplomatically.

In November 1980, Peres met Mitterrand (at that time a presidential candidate), who assured him that France, under Mitterrand, would not supply Iraq with uranium. In December, Begin told Peres that he intended to bomb the Iraqi reactor. In January Peres again met M. Mitterrand, who repeated his promise. On 10 May Peres sent Begin a secret letter in which he stated his opposition to the proposed raid, and urged Begin to wait until after the French election, when Peres' connection to Mitterrand could be put to good use.

When the raid finally came off, Labour was divided and

perplexed as to how to respond. Peres urged that Labour oppose the raid and call it a political grandstand stunt. He was backed by former chief of staff Mota Gur, who called the raid unnecessary and irresponsible, and by Chaim Herzog, who charged that the Iraqis could not possibly produce atomic weapons before 1985. Labour ineptly but insistently tried to pin political motivations on Begin for the raid.

Yet after the raid Begin's ratings in the polls went up in many areas such as the economy and in the overall management of government. On the one issue where the raid would or should have had serious impact – defence – Begin's ratings dropped from 69 per cent to 67 per cent. But experts see the polls as indicating that the voters were beginning to perceive Peres as inept, or as something worse than Begin.

It has been assumed that Peres would not have ordered the attack, yet events, and history, argue otherwise. The military, political and cultural base of Israel is such that it relies heavily on the concept of a very high security margin, the idea that Israel cannot afford to take *any* risks; the Iraqi reactor was perceived as a high risk as long as it existed. The belief is that for Israel to survive surrounded by irresponsible Arab states such as Iraq and Libya, it must have nuclear superiority. This concept has been followed by both the Likud and Labour parties.

The pre-election polls clearly demonstrate that the tougher Begin gets and the closer to his historical image the better are his electoral chances. On 2 June, a poll by a pro-Labour analyst, Dr Peled, clearly demonstrated that despite the narrowing of the gap between Labour and Likud, Labour was still slightly ahead of Likud. The following polls are divided by issues as of 1 June 1981, after the Syrian missile crisis.

The Government's Performance in Security Affairs (1 June 1981)

Percentage of electorate	Jan '81	Missile crisis March '81	May '81
Low	86%	80%	67%
Low performance in general-security issues.	79%	90%	69%

The next poll, by Israel's leading pollster Hanoch Smith on 5 June 1981, after Begin's attack on Chancellor Schmidt of West Germany and President Giscard of France, and after Yoram Aridor's (Treasury Minister) tax relief on televisions and other foreign imported goods, once more demonstrated that the tougher Begin became the higher was his electoral score.

The Government's Performance in Economic Affairs (1 June 1981)

	Jan	Feb	May
Low	83%	75%	66%
Govt. demands too Much from citizen	51%	37%	29%

How Low was Government's Performance (5 June 1981)

	Sept.'79	Sept.'80	Jan.'81	Mar.'81	May '81
Flop	11%	14%	9%	15%	23%
Social	18%	18%	16%	21%	30%
Security	69%	56%	56%	67%	56%
Foreign	74%	37%	30%	20%	41%
General	25%	17%	14%	20%	34%

The end of squabbling represented a rise in the electoral view of better governmental performance, while in the high days during the Egyptian and Camp David negotiations, when Dayan and Weizman consistently challenged Begin, and when Treasury Minister Yigal Horowitz warned: 'I have no money', and continually threatened to resign, the electorate's view was that the governmental performance was low, and that a *correlation* between, on the one hand, strong men and weak government and, on the other, sycophants and strong government became more apparent than ever.

Then came the bombing of the reactor. Smith's poll between 4 and 11 June (the bombing was on 7 June) resulted in a 5 per cent rise · for Likud (who had 40 seats in Knesset). Governmental support for Begin's security policy rose by 11 per cent. The popularity of the government returned to the high days of September 1979 when the strong men were still in government (especially Weizman and Dayan).

The *Jerusalem Post* polls before the raid predicted 45 seats for Likud in late May, 46 in early June, while 42 seats were predicted for Labour in late May and in early June this dropped to 40. The Knesset seats after the raid therefore showed a remarkable turnabout – the first one since March – with Likud scoring 46, and Labour 40.

The Government's Performance (4–11 June 1981)

	High Days of Camp David Sept. '79	Sept.'80	Jan.'81	Mar.'81	May '81 (20–7)	After Bombing June '81
Economic	11%	14%	9%	15%	23%	27%
Social	18%	18%	16%	21%	30%	31%
Security	69%	56%	56%	67%	56%	67%
Foreign	74%	20%	30%	37%	41%	46%
General	25%	17%	14%	20%	34%	38%

The contest from May was no longer between Likud and Labour but between Begin and Peres. Not since David Ben Gurion's early years (1948–56) had the electoral contest been so much of a battle between personalities. It was in fact the first-ever Israeli election to have been fought not on issues but on personalities, despite the fact that issues had seemed crucial and favoured Labour from the middle of 1980 to May 1981: the main ones being Begin's low governmental performance, galloping inflation, Palestine, the defence budget, the quality of life, and ethnic and social issues. Yet none was focused on the crucial months of May–June. As former Foreign Minister Abba Eban said early in June: 'We must zero in on the "Begin Factor".'

Begin's appearance as a demagogue and rebel-rouser, but an effective and supreme electoral campaigner, and his image as a strong man who would teach the terrorist Arabs and the PLO the necessary lessons, were his electoral forte. Charismatic in the eyes of his populist electorate whose excitement and cheers bordered on verbal violence, he was totally detested by the intelligentsia and modern middle-class Israelis.

Yet in the end the 1981 election centred around a personality contrast: Peres won the TV debate – but Begin won the votes.

25

The French Disconnection

France's involvement in the Iraqi nuclear weapons programme did not come about by its desire to contribute to the progress of science and technology.

The Giscard government could apparently not care less if the Middle East and the rest of the world, including France, were embroiled in nuclear war, for the French–Iraqi deal had involved between $1 and 5 billion (depending on the sources), not a small sum even in today's international trade. In addition France was selling no less than a quarter of all its arms to Iraq, with hopes of better deals to come. Finally, they were interested in securing a stable flow of oil from Iraq (France's second-largest supplier).

All these actual and potential deals were *not* changed by the successful Israeli attack.

No doubt this policy was caused many responsible French politicians sleepless nights. Among them was President François Mitterrand, elected 10 May 1981, a month before the raid, who promised Israel's opposition leader on numerous occasions (including February 1981 when they met in Lisbon) to bring French support for the Iraqi nuclear weapons programme to a halt. This intention also became one of his election campaign slogans, no doubt, among other reasons, to attract France's Jewish votes.

Soon after the French election, Mitterrand's new Foreign Minister Claud Cheysson confirmed that the agreements signed by Giscard's government would be fulfilled. This, of course, included French support of the Tammuz project. This about-turn, following so quickly on all Mitterrand's pre-election promises to Israeli leaders and to his own electorate – both in private and in public – *was one of the major considerations that pushed* the Israeli government to make the final decision to destroy the Iraqi reactor.

Now, following the attack, the French government was given an excellent opportunity and a golden excuse to back out of the Iraqi nuclear project. This was not without precedent, as the Israelis were aware: the French under de Gaulle did not hesitate to terminate all their nuclear research collaboration with Israel in 1960, although in this earlier case the French had obtained as much benefit from the Israelis as they had contributed.

A day after the raid the French Prime Minister, M. Mauroy, was quick to condemn the Israeli raid and describe it as 'unacceptable and very serious'. Ten days later, in an interview with the *Washington Post*, Mitterrand sounded more apologetic, though he too denounced the Israeli government's decision to attack the reactor as 'unjustified and alarmist', thus contradicting his own pre-election statements. After all if there was nothing to be alarmed about why had he promised to withdraw French aid from the project? He added that he 'would have seen the Israeli attack in a different light if a real and immediate danger had been facing Israel ... but this, to say the least, was not proved at all.'

He then went on to say that he condemned Israel's leaders – both Begin and his government – rather than Israel's people. He made it clear that France was against imposing sanctions on Israel because the country as a whole should not suffer for the mistakes of their leaders. This was, no doubt, an obvious manoeuvre by the French President to put Begin in a bad light, as part of Mitterrand's attempt to support the election campaign of his old friend Shimon Peres – at the time nearing the end of his election campaign against Begin.

Later on, following Saddam Hussein's speech – in which he demanded that all the developed countries of the world help Iraq and the Arabs obtain nuclear weapons – the French Foreign Minister Cheysson said in an interview on French television (28 July 1981) that for the time being he was not sure whether or not France would again contribute to the Iraqi nuclear 'research' programme (in the same interview he also condemned a statement made earlier the same week that Israel had a very short-term nuclear option).

Following the Israeli raid, the French became more cautious about their involvement in the Iraqi nuclear programme. While France had been a willing provider of Iraq's military needs during its war with Iran and also in the aftermath of that war, it refused to sell Baghdad a similar reactor to the one destroyed. This had, no doubt, a certain impact on the Iraqi decision to turn to the uranium-enrichment rather than the plutonium-separation course during the 1980s, in attempting to pursue a nuclear option. Ironically, the main European assistance to Iraq's build-up of the 'poor man's' substitute for nuclear arms, i.e. biological and chemical weapons, came during the 1980s, and even after 'Desert Storm', from Germany.

France's subdued reaction to the Israeli attack, despite its collaboration in the Iraqi project, might have resulted not only from Israel's having salved the bleeding conscience of the French government[1] and solved a serious dilemma for French decision-makers, but also from the fear that Israel under Begin would not hesitate to publish all the top-secret information available to it, which would show in ugly depth the extent of French support of the Iraqi nuclear weapons programme.

NOTE

1. A French technician – the only foreign victim of the raid – was killed during the bombing of Tammuz. The Israeli government decided two weeks later to pay full and complete compensation to his family (although it was not obliged to do so by international law).

26

The Arab World:
Bridging the Nuclear Gap

Although the Arab world in the summer of 1981 had been, as usual, divided, the Israeli attack on Tammuz reunited it – at least for a short time – in support for Iraq in its humiliation and anger.

Even the Syrian Ba'athist regime, which considers Ba'athist Iraq as one of its main enemies, was suddenly in sympathy with the Iraqis. Damascus Radio called loudly and continually for Arab solidarity to eliminate the 'Zionist entity' in the Middle East. Jordanian reactions were similar, though the Jordanian army had still to explain how Israeli F-16s and F-15s had managed to fly over Jordanian territory undetected by Jordanian radar screens.

From Morocco in the west to Kuwait in the east Israel was condemned again and again for its treacherous attack.

However, we need to take a close look at the reactions of two leading members of the Arab world: Saudi Arabia and Egypt.

Officially both states had joined the campaign against Israel and for Arab solidarity. In Egypt, opposition and coalition members of Parliament reunited again after long months to condemn the Israeli operation. President Sadat called the Israeli ambassador in Egypt, Moshe Sasson, to inform him of his concern. For Sadat, it was also something of a personal insult. Only three days after he had held his meeting with Begin in Ophira the IAF had struck, making him in the eyes of the rest of the Arab world a collaborator in this criminal act. He felt abused by PM Begin and told the Israeli ambassador:

Begin has put me in an intolerable position. I have worked hard to help Israel change from its arrogant and unconquerable image of a long-stretching arm. I wanted to help it acquire the image of a country with which it is possible to live in peace and with which it is possible to sign peace agreements. I have done much to destroy the psychological barrier that prevented the Arab states from even considering the possibility of peace with Israel. Now, your last operation has sabotaged all my efforts and severely hurt what I have tried hard to build in the last three years.

Sadat's words probably explain his immediate reaction to the raid. As one of the more moderate rulers in the Arab world, he saw it in the perspective of the damage it had caused Egyptian–Israeli relations and of the effect it had had on the Arab world concerning his view and attitude towards Israel. But on the other hand the Egyptian president must have also known that the Iraqi nuclear project had also been aimed against Egypt and any other Arab state within the Middle East region, as well as against Israel.

Probably one of the last things he wanted was an Iraqi nuclear bomb, which might threaten any state in conflict with Iraq. Considering this fact, Sadat may have concluded that although the Israeli raid ruined some of his efforts to build a new framework for relations between Israel and the Arab world, it also freed the world from one of the most dangerous developments that could occur, at least in the near future – the Iraqi independent nuclear option. This way of thinking was probably shared by all those in the Egyptian upper ranks who now saw Israel not as the main enemy wanting to occupy its neighbour's territories but as a state which would do everything necessary to ensure its existence.

The Saudis' reaction was officially the same as the rest of the Arab world. It condemned in very sharp words the Israeli attack, calling for Arab solidarity to take the necessary steps against the Jewish state. But there were other reactions, which the radio of Riad never mentioned.

Saudi Arabia's King Khaled who was paying a visit to the UK and other European countries during the time of the Israeli raid, expressed, unofficially of course, some satisfaction with the attack. At a formal lunch in London, other members of the Saudi Royal Family expressed their relief that the Iraqi nuclear project had been ruined. Of course, they were not able to express their feelings too freely – which would have been considered as a betrayal of the Arab cause – but they privately admitted that they had been as worried as much about the Iraqi A-bomb as by the Israeli threat to the Arab world.

This attitude was actually typical of most of the Arab states, who feared the Iraqi plans for hegemony. This threat at least in the short term, was aimed mainly against the Persian Gulf. The Iraq–Iran War was the first step in achieving this hegemony; an independent Iraqi bomb was another means towards this end.

All Arab regimes could have condemned the Israeli attack in the sharpest possible words, but it had served their purposes as much as Israel's. Even so, the Israeli raid on Osirak had also influenced Arab attitudes toward Israel. It was seen as an insult to the whole Arab world, and as an act to perpetuate the gap between modern, sophisticated Israel, which had its own nuclear option, and the Arab world, which would be left way behind without any nuclear option. This was, and probably still is, the genuine feeling and perception of every Arab. The image of the Israeli pilot as Superman – similar to the one that existed following the Six Day War – had also been reinforced upon the Arabs.

The Israeli raid therefore influenced the Arab world as a whole in three different ways. The first is the most superficial: it caused the Arabs to reunite and attempt some kind of Arabic solidarity. Secondly, at a state level, most rulers probably felt great relief after the Israeli raid. A combined Arab effort to achieve the bomb was a legitimate aim for most Arab rulers. An independent Iraqi bomb was a different story entirely. It would threaten each of Iraq's enemies – and Iraq had quite a few of them in the Arab world in the past and at present, and would most probably have more in the future. At this level of national interest, the Israeli attack served the general aims of the Arab rulers.

The last level of influence is the personal one. Here, every Arab citizen felt that the Israeli raid had been a personal humiliation, both for himself and for the Arab nation. The Arabs were frustrated by the Israeli success, which demonstrated once more the large divide between Israeli and Arab abilities and capabilities.

Of course, there were contradictions between these three levels of reaction. While the first, public one, could go together with personal frustration, no Arab ruler would like to see an A-bomb in the hands of his fellow ruler in the neighbouring Arab state. Each of them knows it, but will never admit it. The only way they could all agree to an Arab bomb is by the mutual efforts of all Arab states. But then the question is: who is going to have his finger on the release button of the bomb? Only one person can do it and only one state can own an Arab bomb. Hence, the reaction to the Israeli raid which has left a nuclear monopoly in the Middle East with Israel, also left little chance of a mutual Arab effort to acquire the atomic bomb.

Epilogue to the Second Edition

When the highly secret debate on the bombing of the Iraqi reactor took place in the small group of Israeli policymakers, military generals, intelligence officers and other experts, the pros and the cons of such an act were quite clear. Those who opposed the air raid – policymakers such as Deputy Prime Minister (and former Chief of Staff) Yigael Yadin, or the Director of Military Intelligence, Major-General Yehushua Saguy – maintained that there was no urgent need to carry out the operation and that the cost of any such action would outweigh the benefits. Specifically, they argued, it would take more time before Osirak became 'hot' and that, even if destroyed after it had become operational, the collateral damage would be minimal and probably limited to the nuclear site itself. In addition, they argued that taking an unprecedented act such as the destruction of a nuclear reactor might lead to grave consequences for Israel: the cessation of the peace process with Egypt; the unification of the Arab world against Israel and a possible Arab military response that might escalate into a new war; harsh Soviet anti-Israeli measures, including an increase in military aid to Iraq, Syria and Libya; a possible crisis in Israel's relations with the Reagan administration; and international condemnation. They also feared international pressure on Israel to reveal its own actual nuclear status.

Those who favoured military action, primarily Prime Minister Begin, considered a nuclear Iraq as the most serious threat to the mere existence of the Jewish state. Hence, they were willing to take grave risks in order to prevent it. Begin certainly had another consideration on his mind as well: since he

171

assumed that he was going to lose the forthcoming elections, and since he was certain that the likely new premier, Shimon Peres, was unlikely to take drastic measures against the Iraqi threat, he felt himself committed to destroy Osirak before he left office. He felt so, despite the fact that the professional estimate his intelligence officers gave him was that the destruction of the reactor might buy only limited time, and that in five years Iraq was likely to have a new operational reactor. Buying even a limited amount of time justified in Begin's mind the drastic measures he decided to take. This, in fact, is the main explanation for the timing of operation 'Opera'.

As we have already seen, the short-term price Israel had to pay for the operation was rather minimal. Egypt did not draw back from the peace process; the Arab world avoided any concrete action beyond severe verbal condemnation of the 'Zionist entity'; the USSR did not exploit Arab frustration in order to gain additional strategic assets in the region; international condemnation was limited to words rather than deeds and no serious challenge was made to Israel's nuclear assets by the international community; and the Reagan administration did not take any measures beyond a temporary embargo on the delivery of a number of F-16s.

In early June 1982, Begin, Sharon, Eitan and other supporters of the raid could have looked back at the decision and concluded that the events of the passing year had proved it to be highly justified. It is possible that some of them concluded that the mere use of force was the best means to solve Israeli security challenges. Accordingly, they launched operation 'Peace for Galilee' (later to become the Lebanese war that lasted until 1985) on 6 June 1982, exactly a year after the destruction of Osirak. But while the Israeli invasion of Lebanon proved to be a bitter failure in the long run, the two decades that have passed since operation 'Opera' have showed time and again that this was one of the most successful Israeli military acts, from any perspective.

In retrospect, the destruction of the Iraqi reactor involved two major achievements. The first is the fact that more than 20 years after it lost its main means to become a nuclear power, Saddam Hussein's Iraq is still very far from obtaining the bomb. In this sense, reality showed that even the optimists among the

supporters of the decision to destroy Osirak were not sufficiently optimist: the raid not only bought time, it actually liq-
uidated Iraq's chances of becoming nuclear. Certainly, no one
could have forecast the series of strategic mistakes made by
Saddam Hussein since 1981, which led to this outcome. The
most important of these errors was his 1990 decision to invade
Kuwait, a brutal act that united the world, under American
leadership, against him and made him a pariah. On the eve of
the invasion, Iraq advanced significantly in the uranium-enrichment process and according to some estimates was a year or so
from obtaining a sufficient quantity of enriched uranium to
produce one crude bomb. But during operation 'Desert Storm'
Allied aircraft systematically destroyed Iraq's nuclear infrastructure, leaving Iraq in the aftermath of the war, and the
inspections that followed, lagging far behind in this domain,
even in comparison with its capabilities before the 1981 raid on
Osirak.

The second long-run achievement of operation 'Opera'
involves the radical change of the international community's
approach to the use of force in order to prevent reckless and
brutal leaders from gaining access to nuclear weapons. Begin's
nightmare that Saddam Hussein might use the bomb in order to
destroy Israel, relied not only on memories of the Holocaust,
which shaped his *Weltanschauung*, but also on intelligence
reports that portrayed the strong man of Baghdad as a person
who enjoyed the use of brute force — whether it is the torture
and murder of anyone suspected of undermining his position,
gassing the civilian Kurdish population of Iraq, or the launching of a purely aggressive war against neighboring Iran. In this
sense, Begin and his colleagues made a distinction between
Saddam Hussein and other Arab leaders, and con-cluded that
no stable balance of terror could be obtained with such a terrorist leader.

The international community, led by the United States,
reached this conclusion a decade later, following the Iraqi invasion of Kuwait. Accordingly, it adopted the norm established by
Israel in June 1981, that dangerous leaders such as Saddam
Hussein should not be allowed to possess weapons of mass
destruction (WMD), especially the most dangerous of them all
– nuclear weapons. Two decades after the raid, the events of 11

September 2001 showed how vulnerable open societies had become to other forms of mass violence. Since then, the use of brute military force against any form of major threat to the international community has become an accepted norm rather than the exception, not only by the United States but also by other leading powers, as well as the international community as a whole. The best evidence for this new approach is Resolution 1441 of the UN Security Council of November 2002, that demanded of Iraq complete non-conventional disarmament and warned that if Baghdad would not meet its obligations, it 'will face serious consequences', i.e., the use of military force.

The world still waits to see the outcome of the conflict between the United States and Iraq and the way the Bush administration will deal with other terrorist threats – whether from terrorist organizations or terrorist states. But with the hindsight of more than 20 years, we can already draw one conclusion: to a large extent, the seeds of the present global campaign again the threat of nuclear terrorism were planted on 7 June 1981 by eight daring pilots, who in less than two minutes destroyed Iraq's ambitions to become a nuclear state.

Uri Bar-Joseph
January 2003

APPENDICES

Appendix 1: Israel's Main Decision-makers (1948–81)

Date	Prime Minister	Defence Minister	Commander-in-Chief
May 1948	David Ben Gurion	David Ben Gurion	Yaacov Dory
April 1949	David Ben Gurion	David Ben Gurion	Yigael Yadin
April 1952	David Ben Gurion	David Ben Gurion	Mordechai Maklef
December 1953	Moshe Sharet	Pinhas Lavon	Moshe Dayan
February 1955	Moshe Sharet	David Ben Gurion	Moshe Dayan
November 1955	David Ben Gurion	David Ben Gurion	Moshe Dayan
January 1958	David Ben Gurion	David Ben Gurion	Chaim Laskov
January 1961	David Ben Gurion	David Ben Gurion	Zvi Zur
June 1963	Levi Eshkol	Levi Eshkol	Zvi Zur
January 1964	Levi Eshkol	Levi Eshkol	Yitzhak Rabin
June 1967	Levi Eshkol	Moshe Dayan	Yitzhak Rabin
January 1968	Levi Eshkol	Moshe Dayan	Chaim Bar-Lev
February 1969	Golda Meir	Moshe Dayan	Chaim Bar-Lev
Janurary 1972	Golda Meir	Moshe Dayan	David Elazar
April 1974	Golda Meir	Moshe Dayan	Mordechai Gur
June 1974	Yitzhak Rabin	Shimon Peres	Mordechai Gur
June 1977	Menachem Begin	Ezer Weizman	Mordechai Gur
January 1979	Menachem Begin	Ezer Weizman	Raphael Eitan (Raful)
July 1980	Menachem Begin	Menachem Begin	Raphael Eitan (Raful)
August 1981	Menachem Begin	Ariel Sharon	Raphael Eitan (Raful)

Appendix 2: The Iraqi Nuclear Project

The Iraqi nuclear project involved many names, some of them referring to the same facilities. In order to clarify this a short glossary of the most common names is presented below.

Al Tawita – The site of the Iraqi nuclear project some 20km southeast of Baghdad.

Isis – The original name of Tammuz II reactor.

Osirak – The original name of the Tammuz I reactor.

Osiris – French 70MW nuclear reactor in Saclay near Paris, and exactly the same type as Tammuz I (Osirak), built for the Iraqis.

Project Tammuz 17 – The French-built complex in Al Tawita Included two reactors as well as some labs and other aid facilities needed to operate the complex.

Project 30 July – A laboratory complex for the processing of nuclear fuel (which included a facility for separating plutonium), whose construction by Italian experts had begun in 1978 and whose completion was likewise imminent.

Tammuz I – A 70MW nuclear reactor with a distinct military potential. It was capable of producing approximately 10kg of weapon-grade plutonium per annum. The amount needed for production of one bomb was about 6kg. Originally named Osirak.

Tammuz II – A 1MW nuclear reactor within the project 17 Tammuz. Originally named Isis. Both Tammuz I and II were operated on 93 per cent enriched uranium (weapon-grade uranium).

Appendix 3: Foreign Suppliers of the Iraqi Nuclear Project

Suppliers of Tammuz 17 equipment and services:

CERBAG – A French consortium set up in August 1976 to co-ordinate supplies to the Tammuz 17 project. (CERBAG = Centre d'études et recherche Baghdad.) The members of the consortium were:

I *Technicatome* – The designer of the Tammuz building including both reactors. Supervised erection, assisted in training of Iraqis in France, and was responsible for running of 40 per cent of CERBAG.

II *Bouygues* – Civil engineering and construction. Bouygues set up its own consortium, BBSF, composed of Bouygues Offshore, Boccard, Setip, and Friedlander, to handle plumbing installation. 25 per cent of CERBAG.

III *Société Générale Techniques Nouvelles* – Planning and erection, including running-in of all 'hot' facilities. SGTN transferred air-conditioning systems to Tunzini. 20 percent of CERBAG.

IV *COHSIP* – Installation of control systems and electrical systems. 10 per cent of CERBAG.

V *Constructions Navalset Industrielles de la Méditérranée* – Construction of reactor cores and associated systems, metal coating of reactor pools. 5 per cent of CERBAG.

A second cosortium was set up in the beginning of 1978 on Iraq's request to control the quality of the project, comprising the following members: Institut de protection et de Sureté Nucleaire of the French Atomic Energy Committee (AEC). Bureau Veritas; APPAVE.

Suppliers etc. of 30 July equipment and services:

(1)   CNEN – Consultant to the project.

(2)   *SNIA Techint* – (= SNIA Viscosa and Techint) Planning and pro-duction of most of the components of the project.

(3)   *Incisa, Bergum, Montaggi Industriall Internazionali and Saira* – Civil engineering.

(4)   *Fochi* – Installation.

(5)   *Aermarelli and Aerimpianti* – Ventilation and air-conditioning.

(6)   *Acqua* – Mineral-free water systems.

(7)   *Saima* – Transport of component parts to Iraq.

Appendix 4: Table of Nuclear Development in Middle Eastern Countries

	Status in NPT	Nuclear co-operation agreements	Uranium stock	Research reactors — Active	Research reactors — Under construction	Power reactors — Active	Power reactors — Planned or under construction	Special technology — Enrichment	Special technology — Separation	Standard of manpower	Minimum time to acquire a nuclear bomb	Possible launching systems
Egypt	Signed 1.7.68 Under ratification 1981	USA, France W. Germany	None	WWR-C (Russian-made pressure heavy-water reactor)	None	None	Up to 20 reactors by the year 2000	None	Lab. scale facility unprotected	Not enough	6–10 years	24 SS Scud B, 20 11-28, 20 11-16, 48 Mirage 111 E, 48 Su-20, 35 F-4E Phantom, 24 MiG-23 U, 50 F-16
Iraq	Signed 29.10.69 Ratified 14.3.72	France, Italy Brazil, Pakistan (? unofficial) Belgium (still under negotiation)	12kg 93% enriched U235 330 tons uranium ore (partly enriched to a low grade)	Tammuz I 70MW Tammuz II 1MW 1-R-T 2000 (Soviet) 5MW	None	None	None	Not yet. Under future consideration	Hot facility (lab. scale) cold facility (plant scale). May change to hot in near future	Not enough	2–5 years unless using 93% U235 now in Iraq	30 SS Scud B, 8 Tu-16, 24 Tu-22, 35 Su-20, 24 MiG-23, 24 MiG-25, 15 MiG-27, 30 Mirage F-1EQ (a 3,000km SS missile under planning with Iraqi investment)
Israel	Not a member	USA, RSA (? possible)	Not known	Dimona 24MW (possibly 26MW) Nahal Soneg (1–5MW)	None	None	Under negotiation 2 × 1200MW US power reactors	Not known		Very good	'Bomb in basement' or very immediate option. CIA estimate: 200 warheads	150 F-4 Phantom, 150 Kfir C-2, 50 F-15 Eagle, 40 F-16 Fighting Falcon. Launch missiles, Jericho missiles. Under development: cruise missiles and atomic gun

180

Appendix 4: Continued

	Status in NPT	Nuclear co-operation agreements	Uranium stock	Research reactors Active	Research reactors Under construction	Power reactors Active	Power reactors Planned or under construction	Special technology Enrichment	Special technology Separation	Standard of manpower	Minimum time to acquire a nuclear bomb	Possible launching systems
Libya	Signed and ratified 26.5.75	Argentina, USSR, Pakistan (unofficial)	Unknown but probably 100s tons	10MW Soviet reactor	None	None	440MW Soviet reactor	None	None		10 years unless bought abroad (Pakistan?)	25 SS Scud B, 24 Tu-22, 58 Mirage 5D, 32 Mirage 5DE, 32 Mirage F1 AD, 24 MiG-27, 50 MiG 23M
Pakistan	Not a member	France, UK, Libya (?)	100s tons of U235 ore	Parr	None	Kannup PHWR 125MW	Some reactors planned	Experimental facility in Sihala. Demonstration facility in Kahuta	Unfinished French facility in Charma (may be finished independently). High temperature condition lab. in Islamabad	Very good	Between weeks to one year	15 (B-57B) Canberra, 28 Mirage SPA, 50 Mirage 3EP

181

Appendix 5: A Comparison of Israeli and Iraqi Aircraft

Specification and Data	ISRAELI AIRCRAFT					IRAQI AIRCRAFT				
	F-16 Fighting Falcon	F-15 Eagle	F-4E Phantom	Kfir-C2	A-4M Skyhawk	Mig-23B (Flogger)	Sukhoi SU-17/SU20	MiG-27 (Flogger D and F)	MiG-21MF (Fishbed)	Mirage F-1
Type	Single seat fighter-bomber	Single seat all-weather air superiority fighter	All-weather multi-role fighter bomber	Single seat fighter-bomber	Single seat attack bomber	Single seat all-weather interceptor	Single seat attack and close support aircraft	Single seat tactical attack	Single seat fighter	Single seat multi-mission fighter
General Dimensions	Small sized	Large sized	Large sized	Small sized	Small sized	Medium sized	Medium to large	Medium sized	Small sized	Small to medium
Maximum speed (approx. in mph or kph)	Mach 1.95 1,300mph (2,090kph)	Mach 2.5 1,650mph (2,660kph)	Mach 2.27 1,500mph (2,414mph)	Mach 2.35 1,550mph (2,495kph)	Mach 0.95 45mph (1,100kph)	Mach 2.3 1,520mph (2,445kph)	Mach 2.17 1,432mph (2,305kph)	Mach 1.6 1,055mph (1,700kph)	Mach 2.1 1,285mph (2,070kph)	Mach 2.2 1,450mph (2,335kph)
Initial climb rate (estimated ft/min. or m/min.)	40,000ft/min. (12,200m/min.)	50,000ft/min. (15,240m/min.)	28,000ft/min. (8,534m/min.)	40,000ft/min. (16,765m/min.)	8,840ft/min. (2,572m/min.)		45,275ft/min. (13,800m/min.)		36,090ft/min. (11,000m/min.)	41,930–47,385ft/min. (12,780–14,580m/min.)
Service ceiling	60,000ft (18,300m)	70,000ft (21,000m)	60,000ft (19,685m)	55,000ft (12,200m)	49,000ft (14,935m)	61,000ft (18,600m)	59,050ft (18,000m)	50,000ft. (15,250m.)	59,050ft (18,000m)	65,000ft (20,000m)

Appendix 5: Continued

Specification and Data	ISRAELI AIRCRAFT					IRAQI AIRCRAFT				
	F-16 Fighting Falcon	F-15 Eagle	F-4E Phantom	Kfir-C2	A-4M Skyhawk	Mig-23B (Flogger)	Sukhoi SU-17/SU20	MiG-27 (Flogger D and F)	MiG-21MF (Fishbed)	Mirage F-1
Range on internal fuel in interception mission	1,300 miles (2,100km)	1,200 miles (1,930km)	1,750 miles (2,817km)	700 miles (1,125km)	920 miles (1,480km)	combat range hi-lo-hi 600 miles (966km)	combat radius with 4,400lb or 2,000kg 391 miles (630km)	with bombs and one fuel tank 600 miles (950km)	range high and on internal fuel 683 miles (1,100km)	with hi-lo-hi 500 miles (900km)
Maximum tactical load limit	15,200lb (6,895kg)	12,000lb (5,443kg)	16,000lb (7,257kg)	8,500lb (3,855kg)	9,155lb (4,115kg)	11,000lb (5,000kg)	11,000l (5,000kg)	4,200l (1,900kg)	3,500lb (1,500kg)	8,820lb (4,000kg)

All the data are for maximum performance parameters. In reality most military aircraft almost never fly at their maximum speed – and if they do, they can stay airborne for a much shorter time due to the high rate of fuel consumption. US-made aircraft normally had overall a much longer range of operation than tactical fighter-bombers made in the Soviet Union and France. In addition, they were usually equipped with better navigation aids and more accurate bombing equipment. The F-15 and F-16 (which saw their first battle operation by the Israeli Air Force over Iraq on 7 June 1981) were a generation ahead of all the Soviet or French aircraft currently in operation. While this cannot be deduced simply from their performance parameters such as maximum speed, or range, they had a much higher (or faster) rate of climb and were much more manoeuvrable than older generation fighter bombers. They could, so to speak, 'turn on a dime', i.e. could execute much tighter manoeuvres.

It must also be remembered that the *lower* aircraft fly and for longer ranges, the more fuel and the less bomb loads they can carry. This was the situation the Israelis had to face when planning the raid on the Iraqi reactor (see text). Normally the solution is to carry long-range missiles as well as the heaviest bomb payloads and refuel in the air shortly after take-off.

A great advantage for aircraft – seen as particularly important by the Israelis in light of their experience during the Yom Kippur War (1973) – is the small size of fighter-bombers, which makes them more difficult to trace visually or by radar and which makes them a smaller target for all sorts of anti-aircraft fire.

The Israelis enjoyed three major advantages: firstly, they were more experienced pilots than the Iraqis – perhaps the most important condition for success, i.e., more important than the quality of the aircraft; secondly, they had the advantage of surprise (as described in the text); and thirdly, they had the advantage of better aircraft.

The Iraqis on the other hand were less experienced, and directed their attention primarily toward Iran; as a result of the continued war with Iran, their air force had probably been considerably reduced and was in need of spare part maintenance, etc.